TWAYNE'S UNITED STATES AUTHORS SERIES

Sylvia E. Bowman, *Editor*

INDIANA UNIVERSITY

Richard Henry Dana, Jr.

RICHARD HENRY DANA

Richard Henry Dana, Jr.

by ROBERT L. GALE
University of Pittsburgh

 143

Twayne Publishers, Inc.   : :   New York

MANUFACTURED IN THE UNITED STATES OF AMERICA

For Christine

RICHARD HENRY DANA

by

ROBERT L. GALE

This study is the first book on Richard Henry Dana, Jr. (1815-1882), to relate all the major events of his life and to evaluate his writings. Dana was a curious mixture: a realist and a romantic, a sailor and a Harvard graduate, a defender of the oppressed who earned huge fees for admiralty work, a brilliant politician who refused to campaign realistically, a devoted husband and father who once took a 433-day vacation alone, a distinguished editor who was once sued for plagarism, and a Boston brahmin who died in Rome. Given these elements, he inevitably felt dissatisfied with his life.

Ironically, the one accomplishment by which he is known today is *Two Years Before the Mast*, which he once dismissed as "a boy's work." It beautifully reflects its author. Realistically told, and reflecting joy in hard, common work, *Two Years Before the Mast* is also an account which challenges romantic archetypal criticism. In the present study, *Two Years Before the Mast* is analyzed in detail for its narrative skill, its structure and form, its rhetorical features, and its tone.

Dana also wrote *The Seaman's Friend*, a manual for sailors; *To Cuba and Back*, an account of his vacation to Cuba and an analysis of its customs and institutions; *Speeches in Stirring Times*

and *Letters to a Son*, on a wide variety of subjects; and a 600,000-word secret *Journal*, of great interest. All of these works are studied in detail in the present book.

Preface

THIS STUDY IS THE first book which attempts not only to tell the story of the life of Richard Henry Dana, Jr., but also to evaluate all of his major writings. His famous *Two Years Before the Mast* has so long overshadowed the man that few people are aware of his activities apart from it. But the truth is that, in addition to his classic of the sea, Dana wrote a popular sailor's manual, an influential book about Cuba, several stirring political and juridical speeches, many splendid letters, and an autobiographical sketch to precede a two-decade *Journal* which only recently has been published in full.

Dana himself is partly responsible for critical neglect, since he never realized that he had literary genius and, instead of developing it, prided himself first, last, and always on being a lawyer. Also a minor politician who aspired to be a major one, even a statesman, he was constantly frustrated in this ambition, as though by a malignant fate. In addition, he wanted to be a gentlemanly scholar of international law and the historian of his distinguished family, of which he was almost irrationally proud. Death cut him off somewhat prematurely and hence blocked him from these goals. It is ironic, therefore, that *Two Years Before the Mast* is alone responsible for his renown; and it is so in spite of the fact that Dana sought to outgrow his literary masterpiece which, late in his life, he called "a boy's work."

The present study of Dana is in two parts. Chapters 1, 2, 3, 4, and 5 recount the story of his life, which is noteworthy for two main reasons: (1) for a Brahmin's career, it was unusually varied and exciting in spots; and (2) because it was a Brahmin's, it is dramatically conservative and full of missed opportunities. But Dana emerges as a rather inspiring figure—moral, self-critical, public-spirited, energetic, articulate, and noble in adversity. Chapters 6, 7, and 8 consider Dana's literary works. *Two Years Before the Mast* is analyzed as to narrative, structure and form, rhetoric, tone, and mythic qualities, and is then compared to several other American journey books. Next considered are Dana's lesser works, which include *The Seaman's Friend, To Cuba and*

Back: A Vacation Voyage, Speeches in Stirring Times and Letters to a Son, and his *Journal.* Chapter 9 is a brief summation.

Every serious student of Dana must acknowledge his debt to four scholars. Charles Francis Adams, Jr., the brother of Henry Adams, read law in Dana's office for a time and then much later, in 1890, published a biography of the man. Then professional interest in Dana subsided for several decades until, in 1936, James D. Hart wrote a distinguished Harvard University doctoral dissertation on the life of Dana, drawing on Charles Francis Adams but going far beyond him and making modern critical use of masses of additional material and presenting many fresh insights. Next, in 1958, Robert F. Lucid wrote an admirably thorough University of Chicago doctoral dissertation called "The Composition, Reception, Reputation, and Influence of *Two Years Before the Mast.*" Neither of these fine dissertations has been published, although four or five useful articles in journals grew out of them. Finally, also in 1958, Samuel Shapiro wrote a history dissertation at Columbia University on Dana, necessarily stressing Dana's part in the Free Soil movement and the early years of the Republican party, his opposition to progressive change, and his political ambitions; Professor Shapiro properly slights Dana's literary side. Shapiro's biography was published in 1961 and is especially valuable for literature students because of its many bibliographical leads.

Aside from the work of Adams, Hart, Lucid, and Shapiro, worthwhile critical commentary on Dana is almost nonexistent. While *Two Years Before the Mast* continues to enjoy its immortality— it is never out of print—serious scholars of American literature have almost uniformly ignored its artistry and the man behind it. Professor Thomas Philbrick's work on James Fenimore Cooper and sea fiction intelligently places Dana in the mainstream of American Realism. But much work remains to be done before Dana will be clearly seen for what he was, a distinguished if imperfect early Realist who was as honest with his material as Ernest Hemingway ever was. And in addition, Dana was a cunning jurisprudential authority, a vigorous forensic stylist, an engaging travel-literature writer, and a diarist whose worth is only beginning to be appreciated.

University of Pittsburgh   ROBERT L. GALE

Acknowledgments

IT IS A pleasure to acknowledge my indebtedness to Professor Robert F. Lucid of the University of Pennsylvania. Even while he was preparing the massive Dana *Journal* for publication, he placed a transcript of its half-million words at my disposal—a rare act of scholarly generosity. Also he has permitted me to quote from his Dana dissertation. In addition, I am grateful for the many kindnesses of the following persons and institutions: Professor James D. Hart of the University of California, for permission to quote from his Dana dissertation; Mr. Richard D. Lewis, editor of the Ward Ritchie Press, Los Angeles, California, and Mr. John Haskell Kemble, editor of the recent and superb Ward Ritchie Press edition of Dana's *Two Years Before the Mast,* for permission to quote extensively from it; Mr. Robert F. Metzdorf, editor of Dana's *Autobiographical Sketch,* for permission to quote from it; Mr. Stephen T. Riley, Director of the Massachusetts Historical Society, for permission to read and quote from Dana's *Journal,* the copyright of which the Society retains, and for the privilege of reading and excerpting from masses of unpublished Dana family material which his staff efficiently placed before me; Professor Samuel Shapiro of the University of Notre Dame, and Mr. Lyle Blair, editor of the Michigan State University Press, for permission to quote from Shapiro's *Dana;* Mrs. Barbara Miller Solomon, Director of the Women's Archives, Radcliffe College, for permission to quote from the diaries of Dana's wife Sarah Watson Dana; Mr. Thomas De Valcourt, Curator of the Longfellow House, Cambridge, Massachusetts, for the privilege of perusing quantities of Dana family papers and for quoting from a letter by James Russell Lowell to Dana; and Mr. Thomas J. Wilson, Director of the Harvard University Press, publishers of Dana's *Journal,* for permission to quote from it. Unfortunately, I completed this study of Dana before the *Journal* was published. Therefore, I cite it by date only.

I am also indebted to the many skillful librarians of the University of Pittsburgh Library, the Carnegie Public Library of Pittsburgh, the Houghton Library and the Widener Library of Harvard University, and the University of Sheffield. In addition,

I deeply appreciate sabbatical time and grant-in-aid funds given to me by the English Department and the Division of the Humanities of the University of Pittsburgh, and a travel grant given to me by the Office of Cultural and Educational Exchange of the University of Pittsburgh, all of which enabled me to complete this book. And finally, my sincere gratitude to Professor Sylvia E. Bowman for her editorial skill and tact.

Contents

Chronology

1815   Richard Henry Dana, Jr., born August 1 in Cambridge, Massachusetts, second of four children of Richard Henry (died 1879) and Ruth Charlotte Smith Dana (died 1822); the other children: Ruth Charlotte Dana (1814-1901), Edmund "Ned" Trowbridge Dana (1818-69), and Susan Dana (1820-22).

1823-   Attended various schools in Cambridgeport, Westford,
1831   and Cambridge.

1831-   Attended Harvard College; suspended March to Septem-
1833   ber, 1832; forced by failing eyesight following measles in beginning of junior year to discontinue.

1834   August 14, left Boston aboard brig *Pilgrim,* rounding Cape Horn early in November on way to California.

1835   January 14, anchored at Santa Barbara, California; began working at hide-droghing and related tasks there and at San Francisco, Monterey, Los Angeles, and San Diego.

1836   May 8, left California aboard ship *Alert,* rounding Cape Horn mid-July and arriving at Boston September 20; began to attend Episcopal Church, Boston; re-entered Harvard in December.

1837   Graduated with Class of 1837; entered Dane Law School, Harvard.

1838   Confirmed in Episcopal Cathedral Church of St. Paul, Boston, in April.

1839   January, appointed instructor in elocution at Harvard (resigned February, 1840).

1840   Left Law School in March to enter Boston law office for experience in practice; September, was admitted to bar and opened law office at 20 Court Street, Boston, and soon began to do well; *Two Years Before the Mast* published mid-September.

1841   August 25, married Sarah "Sally" Watson, in Hartford, Connecticut (six children: Sarah Watson Dana, June, 1842; Ruth Charlotte Dana, June, 1844; Elizabeth Ellery Dana, April, 1846; Mary Rosamund Dana, September, 1848; Richard Henry Dana, III, January, 1851; and Angela

Henrietta Channing Dana, February, 1857); *The Seaman's Friend* published October; December, began keeping *Journal* (until September, 1860).

1842 Began public lecturing (continued until 1856).

1844 January, moved office to 30 Court Street, Boston.

1846 Took Francis Edward Parker as law partner (until 1861).

1848 August, attended National Free Soil Convention at Buffalo.

1851 Was involved in "Rescue Trials" of several persons accused of rescuing Shadrach, apprehended fugitive slave (continued this work into 1852).

1852 Moved into his own home, 4 Berkeley Street, Cambridge.

1853 May to August, participated in Massachusetts Constitutional Convention at Boston.

1854 May and June, unsuccessfully defended fugitive slave Anthony Burns; was assaulted at night by hired thug for doing so.

1855 Summer, joined Saturday Club as one of its original members.

1856 July and August, vacationed in England and France; October, moved office to Brattle and Court Streets, Boston.

1859 February 12 to March 17, traveled to Cuba for vacation. *To Cuba and Back* published April or May; July, had severe fit induced by overwork; July 20, started trip around world (ending September 27, 1860).

1861 April, was appointed by President Lincoln to be United States District Attorney for District of Massachusetts (until September, 1866).

1863 February, successfully presented federal position concerning "Prize Cases" before Supreme Court.

1866 Was granted degree of Doctor of Laws by Harvard; edited Wheaton's *Elements of International Law*, published July; vacationed abroad; October, was sued by William Beach Lawrence, Wheaton's previous editor, for infringement of copyright (case dragged on until 1880); resumed practice of law, in Court Street office (until 1878); was elected to represent Cambridge in Massachusetts Legislature (reelected 1867).

1868 Unsuccessfully opposed Benjamin Franklin Butler for election to House of Representatives; earned large retainers for admiralty work.

Chronology

1870   Impaired health led to brief vacation in Europe.

1871   Moved residence to 361 Beacon Hill, Boston.

1876   President Grant's nomination of Dana in March to be ambassador to England was blocked in Senate by political and personal enemies; delegate-at-large to Republican Convention in Cincinnati.

1877   Failed to obtain federal employment through President Hayes.

1878   Retired from law to write book on international law; lived pleasantly in Paris and studied casually.

1879   July, settled deceased father's estate; August, participated in final hearings of plagiarism case of *Lawrence v. Dana;* September, returned to Paris.

1880-   Lived, studied, and vacationed in France, Switzerland,
1882   and Italy; began in Rome, December, 1881, to write book on international law.

1882   January 6, died in Rome; was buried in Protestant Cemetery there.

CHAPTER *1*

The Years Before
Two Years Before the Mast

A S THE SUNLIGHT faded over Boston Harbor on September 20, 1836, a bronzed young sailor of twenty-one stood on the deck of the *Alert*. His delight at being home again after two years at sea and in remote California must have been tempered by several apprehensions. What should he do now? Let way lead on to way, or retrace a few steps and get back to the more worn path? Visit a melancholy home for a short time and then seek new adventure, or return to Harvard College and a safer course of action?

Richard Henry Dana, Jr., did not know it, but he was at a crossroads, like many another nineteenth-century American writer or aspirant to literary fame. In 1818, Irving decided to stop trying to represent a failing family business and instead continue writing; in 1820, Cooper accepted his wife's challenge and began writing novels; and in 1832, Emerson left the Unitarian ministry to prepare for the career of a man of letters. In 1847, Melville decided to follow two relatively easy literary successes with philosophically deeper fiction; in 1864, Howells left the consular service in Venice and came home to write; and in 1875, James determined to live permanently in Europe.

But when Dana listened in 1836 to his conservative inner voice, composed of family and religious and academic strains, he turned his back on liberating adventure and chose a partially stifling course of action which made him periodically uneasy for the remainder of his life. It was an awesome moment, and the young man must have unconsciously felt that he was in the eye of a storm whose contending winds would soon try to push him in opposing directions. Otherwise, how can we explain his mood of

17

seeming indifference upon returning to his home? As Dana tells us at the end of his *Two Years Before the Mast*:

> So much did we feel ourselves to be already at home, by anticipation, that our plain supper of hard bread and salt beef was barely touched; and many on board, to whom this was the first voyage, could scarcely sleep. As for myself, by one of those anomalous changes of feeling of which we are all the subjects, I found myself in a state of indifference, for which I could by no means account. A year before, while carrying hides on the coast, the assurance that in a twelve-month we should see Boston, made me half wild; but now that I was actually there, and in sight of home, the emotions which I had so long anticipated feeling, I did not find, and in their place was a state of very nearly entire antipathy.[1]

I *Forerunners*

One cause of Dana's antipathy in Boston Harbor might well have been his illustrious forebears. Many of them would have been a challenge for any young fellow. The first American Dana was also a Richard, born in England about the time Shakespeare died. He had come to Boston about 1640, married, prospered, sired ten children, and died in 1690 leaving an estate of three hundred pounds, mostly in land. His son Daniel Dana (1663-1749) in turn married and had eight children. One of them, another Richard (1700-72), graduated from Harvard College, taught in the Roxbury Latin School, married well, and entered politics; as a crusty old judge, he did his bit on the eve of the Revolution to foment rebellion against the British; and, if he had not died in 1772, he might be as well known today as his crony Sam Adams. Judge Dana and his well-to-do Cambridgeport wife had five children, including Francis Dana (1743-1811), who was also a Harvard graduate, and in addition a lawyer, a delegate to the Continental Congress, an unrecognized minister to Russia under President George Washington, a wealthy Congressman from Massachusetts, and finally a supreme court justice of that state. This able man combined political acumen and a variety of activities in a way which his grandson Richard Henry Dana, Jr., longed all his life to emulate.

Two of old Judge Francis Dana's six children are of special

18

concern to us. One, Francis Dana, Jr., our Dana's uncle, frittered away huge sums of money building docks and wharves along the Charles River in an impractical effort to make the ancestral Dana lands from Harvard Yard to the river more accessible to mercantile interests. The second was Dana's father, Richard Henry Dana, Sr. (1787-1879). He demonstrated spirit enough while at Harvard to be expelled in 1807 for his activities during a student rumpus. He was admitted to the Massachusetts bar in 1811, and two years later he married for love rather than to improve the financial and social image of the Danas, as most of his ancestors had done since the end of the seventeenth century.

The young woman he chose was Ruth Charlotte Smith of nearby Providence. Charming and gentle but not of good health, she died in 1822 after bearing her melancholy husband four children—Ruth Charlotte (1814-1901), Richard Henry (1815-82), Edmund "Ned" Trowbridge (1818-69), and Susan (1820-22).[2] The three surviving children always revered their mother's memory; and, twenty years after her death, young Dana wrote about her in his *Autobiographical Sketch*:

> I was six years old when my mother died. This event made a deep & solemn impression upon me. The effect of it was aided by other causes, among which was the sacredness attached to it & to her memory by us all, so great that up to this time, a period of 20 years, her name has never been mentioned among us or anything nearly connected with her alluded to, except in the most perfect privacy, & then with a solemnity & awe like that with which we should have gone down into her tomb. . . . When we were mere children, our father used to take us upon his knees of a Sunday afternoon, after church, & having first read some passage of scripture & talked a little upon religion & God & our Savior, then speak to us of our mother, her character, her dying words, her wishes & prayers for us. This was always a time of full hearts & of tears among us. (33) *

Dana's father was a somewhat more palpable influence. Though nominally a lawyer, he preferred to live on his shrunken patri-

---

* All parenthetical references in this chapter are to Richard Henry Dana, Jr., *Autobiographical Sketch (1815-1842)*, ed. Robert F. Metzdorf (Hamden, Connecticut, 1953).

mony as a half-Calvinist and half-romantic man of letters. He helped found the *North American Review* and earned a footnote immortality by doubting that the sonorous blank verse of the anonymously submitted "Thanatopsis" could have been written on this side of the Atlantic.[3] William Cullen Bryant insisted that it had been, and the two men became lifelong friends. Bryant encouraged the elder Dana to write reams of mediocre Romantic verse, the best of which is in the now seldom-read "Buccaneer" and "Little Beach-Bird."

The elder Dana's literary criticism has more value. It includes essays on non-dramatic English literature, lectures on English dramatists, and reviews of such American men of letters as Washington Irving, Charles Brockden Brown (whom Dana knew), and Washington Allston (Dana's brother-in-law). Dana's attack on Alexander Pope and his general preference for Wordsworthian Romanticism over Neo-Classicism led to his ouster from the editorial board of the conservative *North American Review,* whereupon Dana moved temporarily to New York and founded the short-lived and costly paper *The Idle Man* (1821-22). The most revealing thing about that periodical was its name, which beautifully sums up its founder. In fact, James Russell Lowell, a childhood chum of the man's children, says as much with wicked wit in his *Fable for Critics*:

> Here comes Dana, abstractedly loitering along
> Involved in a paulo-post-future of song,
> Who'll be going to write what'll never be written
> Till the Muse, ere he think of it, gives him the mitten,—
> Who is so well aware of how things should be done,
> That his own works displease him before they're begun,—
> . . . .
> That he once was the Idle Man none will deplore,
> But I fear he will never be anything more . . .[4]

If the elder Dana had shown one tenth the ambition and energy that his son possessed, and if he had tried to polish the family name instead of basking in it, the life of his son and namesake would have been a happier one. But, retiring into melancholia at the age of thirty-five, Richard Henry Dana, Sr., became an officious parasite and yet a curiously respected source of unconscious frustration to his vigorous son.

20

II *School Days, School Days*

Richard Henry Dana, Jr., was born August 1, 1815, in the Dana family house on Green Street in Cambridge, Massachusetts. His first years were full of adventuresome, independent play, in spite of the well-intentioned warnings of his frail mother and his gloomy father. He went whortle-berrying, followed soldiers and showmen and cattle, got into squabbles, and frolicked in water and woods. His father later told him that he often wordlessly worried about the boy but still encouraged him to be self-reliant and natural; "for he . . . always . . . felt [Dana later wrote] that a good constitution, a strong & active body, & elasticity of mind & spirits, if the ordinary & necessary school drilling & general information were secured & the moral & religious character impressed, would be of far more value than that little advance in learning that might be got by time taken from play & exercise" (32).

A year after his mother's death, Dana began attending various schools in the general vicinity of Boston. The first of these was managed in Cambridgeport by Samuel Barrett, later a Boston Unitarian minister. This dark, austere man punished every misdemeanor with two to two dozen blows from a pine ferrule on the inky palms of his wretched charges. He may have instilled the beginnings of a lifelong love of Latin in Dana, but he made himself mainly loathsome to the boy for his specialty of ear-pulling. He once tore Dana's ear and made it bloody when he dragged the boy by the ear over the benches for chuckling irrepressibly. Dana probably had this experience in mind when in 1860, having visited a scrubby but gay little school in Hakodadi, Japan, he noted in his *Journal*: "The boys looked very lively & happy—a contrast with the stupor of an 8 year old school, when I was of that age."[5]

Outlasting two masters at the Cambridgeport school, the sturdy lad next studied at home and recited to a minister; then he was sent to Westford, twenty-five miles northwest of Cambridge, a distance that required him to board away from home for the first time. He was at first subject to attacks of homesickness, and learned little and daydreamed much during his sixteen-month Westford tenure. Home again in the fall of 1825, Dana was sent to yet another private school in Cambridge by his peculiar father, who actually wrote about the boy to a friend as follows:

If I understand Richard, he is a boy of excellent principles even now. I am afraid he is too sensitive for his own happiness; yet he is generally cheerful and ready for play, and is a boy of true spirit. After all, I never think of him without some touch of melancholy, and with an impression that if he lives he will not be happy; and so constant is this feeling in me whenever he comes before my mind, that should he die early, tho' it would be a sad thing to part with him, my first and last thought of him would be, he has escaped the evil to come. I know this is a weakness in me. But when have I been other than a creature of weakness and folly?[6]

After a short time Dana transferred back to Cambridge, and this time he came under the sway of a young Harvard graduate whom he later described as "since known as a writer & lecturer upon what is called the transcendental philosophy . . . a very pleasant instructor . . . , although he had not system or discipline enough to ensure regular & vigorous study. I have always considered it fortunate for us [Dana felt obliged to add] that we fell into the hands of more systematic & strict teachers, though not so popular with us, nor perhaps so elevated in their habits of thought as Mr. E" (44). "Mr. E." was a young fellow named Ralph Waldo Emerson.

Two personnel changes later, Dana was under the more systematic ministrations of one Reverend William H. Sandford, whom he later called the best teacher he ever had, "Mr. E." notwithstanding. Using no corporal punishment, Sandford kept his Latin and Greek scholars in line by noting on the spot all infractions of his strict regulations and by listening to all excuses at a set time after school (45). Next came a pleasant, cultivated teacher, who, as Dana recalled, "lacked the tact, efficiency & system of his predecessor, & the school fell away under his dynasty" (46). Dana always seems to have set as an ideal a pedagogical appeal to honor but within inflexibly set behavioral limits.

His next teacher, Horatio Wood, was his worst. He lasted only two weeks, and Dana was the cause of his being released. Stationed near the hot stove for some offense, Dana soon became faint, asked permission to go home, was refused, but went anyway. His father, distressed by his appearance, kept him home for the rest of the day and sent him back the following morning with

a written excuse. Wood became enraged, intimated that Dana had
been shamming, charged him with leaving the day before without
permission, and—in the victim's vivid words—

> . . . calling me out, took his ferrule & ordered me to put out
> my left hand. . . . Upon this hand, he inflicted six blows
> with all his strength, & then six upon the right hand. I was
> in such a phrenzy of indignation at his injustice . . . that I
> could not have uttered a word, for my life. I was too small &
> slender to resist, & could show my spirit only by fortitude.
> He called for my right hand again & gave six more blows in
> the same manner, & then six more upon the left. My hands
> were swollen & in acute pain, but I did not flinch nor show a
> sign of suffering. He was determined to conquer & gave six
> more blows upon each hand, with full force. Still there was
> no sign from me of pain or submission. I could have gone to
> the stake for what I considered my honour. The school was in
> an uproar of hissing & scraping & groaning, & the master
> turned his attention to the other boys & let me alone. (47)

The tortured lad did all that was in his puny power to do: lacking the strength to challenge Wood personally, he went to the
trustees and reported his treatment. Wood was discharged.

When Dana turned fourteen, he became a day student at a
highly regarded but stultifying preparatory school in Cambridge
run by one William Wells, British born but Harvard educated.[7]
The curriculum included Latin, Greek, French, history, mathematics, and flogging. Dana's description of the place is most depressing:

> The school-room was the only room in which the boys could
> be, except when in bed, by day or night, . . . & in which
> their characters & habits were formed. This room was oblong,
> rather small for the number of boys it was to accommodate,
> with a stove in the middle, & but one light in the evening
> for all the boys, & that a lamp fastened to the wall higher
> than the boys' heads, & of such a kind & so placed that but
> two or three boys could read by it at the same time. . . .
> Those boys who passed several years at this school before
> entering college, went to college the most ignorant young
> men upon all subjects of literature & of that knowledge ac-
> quired through books & the society of educated persons, &
> not necessarily connected with their Latin, Greek & mathe-
> matics, of any who are able to get for themselves what is

commonly called a liberal education. . . . They were inferior
. . . also in the spirits [sports?] & athletic exercises of boys.
(51)

Wells's school was fortunately also the scene of high-jinks
which could have inspired Tom Sawyer. Dana's cohorts included
James Russell Lowell and Thomas Wentworth Higginson, who
records in his autobiography *Cheerful Yesterdays* that a fellow
sufferer called the school "hell." But Higginson relates that they
played ball and other running games, were once entertained by
knife fights between some Puerto Rican students, and amused
themselves at the expense of the unwary by perforating each of
the school seats "with two small holes for needles, to be worked
by a pulley, for a sudden impaling of a fellow student, or even
of the mathematics usher."[8] Dana remembered longer the dull
little boys who wept over their incomprehensible lessons. "One
of them [he records] was weeks & weeks upon a few pages of
his Latin grammar, which he had blotted with tears & blackened
with his fingers, until they were barely legible. That boy generally cried for a quarter to a half of an hour every half-day, over
his lesson" (52-53).

Of the schooling to which Dana was exposed, he joyfully re-
calls in favor of it only that an "uncommon gentlemanly spirit
. . . prevailed among the scholars. . . . A boy lost caste by being
vulgar & profane. It was looked upon as ungentlemanly & low
bred. . . . A high sense of honor & a certain pride of personal character was the *esprit du corps*. A mean action, vulgar or indecent
language, coarse or illmannered behavior, put a boy down in a
position from which he rarely & with difficulty recovered" (49).
Dana's scholarly diet was dead languages, warmed over for the
most part by intellectually dying masters—a poor preparation for
his life in his century. His only teacher of whom history has taken
note, Emerson, he saw fit to criticize for lacking system and
discipline. But Professor James D. Hart, Dana's ablest biographer,
says flatly that it was unfortunate that Dana was not Emerson's
pupil longer, for "certainly he there lost the opportunity to be
molded for his own age under the tutelage of the man whose
philosophy was to be so important in New England during Dana's
maturity."[9]

When Dana entered Harvard College in 1831, he knew some

24

Greek and Latin, a little theoretical mathematics, some history, and some geography. As a young man, he evidenced a stiff stoicism and a priggish pride in a family fast becoming content to rest on its once-great name.

III *Harvard College*

In the 1830's Harvard College was beginning to feel the effects of the new administrative broom wielded by President Josiah Quincy, who personally quizzed young Dana in Greek, Latin, history, and geography before admitting him. Quincy's more important duties and accomplishments included fighting for religious and academic freedom, and for material expansion at Harvard. Against attacks on the tolerant college for what its opponents considered treachery to Calvinism, its Unitarian sectarianism, and even its atheism, "Old Quin" stood firm. He proudly pointed to these facts: his students were free to attend any Sunday service that they or their parents chose; morning and evening prayers were in force daily but were little more than an ineffective roll call; and of his staff of fourteen teachers and officers, six were Unitarians, three were Roman Catholics, and the other five included an Episcopalian, a Calvinist, a Lutheran, a Quaker, and a Sandemanian.[10]

Quincy regularly supported faculty members whose extracurricular activities included espousing unpopular social and even political causes such as Abolition. In fact, he once wrote eloquently on the subject of religious and political freedom for his teachers:

> The duty of considering science and learning as an independent interest of the community, begins to be very generally felt and acknowledged. Both in Europe and America attempts are making to rescue the general mind from the vassalage in which it has been held by sects in the church, and by parties in the state; giving to that interest, as far as possible, a vitality of its own, having no precarious views in politics or religion; and, for this purpose, to place it like a fountain opened in regions far above those in which the passions of the day struggle for ascendency,—to which all may come to gain strength and be refreshed, but whose waters none shall be permitted to disturb by their disputes or exclusively to preoccupy for purposes of ambition.[11]

But in spite of all his principles and his accomplishments, "Old Quin" was energetically loathed by the entire student body, including Dana. Quincy enforced a reformed grading system which demanded recitation and discouraged initiative, and he personally averaged all students' grades weekly. In addition, although students a little after Dana's time were permitted some choice of subjects, the grading system penalized them for exercising that freedom and made it difficult for even the best young scholars to be among the top ten students without adhering to the old curriculum. Quincy also herded his spirited charges away from fights with townies and otherwise ruled them with the same rigid hand that he had employed when he was the mayor of Boston earlier. In the spring of 1834, admitting that he could not ferret out the students responsible for an orgy of window-breaking and furniture-smashing on campus, he expelled the entire sophomore class and turned all suspicious students over to an inquisitorial but ineffectual county grand jury for grilling.[12]

Dana was not involved in this altercation because he was then still suffering the after-effects of the measles which weakened his eyesight and forced him out of Harvard. But he was caught in the middle of an earlier fracas which Quincy handled with equal tactlessness. In February, 1831, Quincy evidently discharged a charity scholar for refusing to tell grand-jury investigators what he knew about a minor infraction of regulations by another student. Dana and his classmates expressed sympathy for their hapless colleague in the form of hisses, groans, and foot-scrapings at assembly. The authorities hinted to Richard Henry Dana, Sr., that, if his son simply stayed away from his unruly friends for a while, he would not be expelled. But, when the lad explained to his father that injustice was being offered his class and that a point of honor was involved, he was allowed to pursue his rebellious course, which led on March 2 to his six-months' suspension—spent at Andover, Massachusetts.

Dana regarded his exile from Harvard as a positive boon. He had done nothing dishonorable; he was something of a martyr, although one surrounded by legions of his peers. And he passed into the care of a brilliant young scholar, Leonard Woods, Jr., then of the rather Calvinistic Andover Theological Seminary and later president of Bowdoin College. Under this man, Dana began a course of rigorous private study, including Greek, Latin, German, and—through a friend of Woods—advanced geometry. This supervised program, not cursed by the requirement of daily recitation, encouraged him to progress as rapidly as he wished. Free though Harvard had been of religious pressure, it was still palely Unitarian; so Woods's more liberal Congregationalism was another welcome change. Actually reluctant to return to Harvard, Dana wrote in mid-August: ". . . having lived for 6 months in this one spot, and in the same course of life, it has come to feel to me, as it were, like another home. If it were not for the family at home, I should look upon Cambridge as a place I had once visited. There is no society there which is at all interesting, and nothing to benefit one at all."[13]

Seemingly, Dana attended Harvard too early during Quincy's reign to benefit from the changes beginning to be planned. Because he was mindful that, since 1826, the top ten scholars of each class were publicly praised at commencement, Dana would conservatively have avoided point-losing elective courses anyway. And, unlike Thoreau, who arrived at Harvard in 1833 and soon began studying Oriental classics in his abundant free time, Dana used the burgeoning Harvard library but little; in fact, the records indicate that he checked out only ten books in his first three years and only eleven more after his return from the sea.[14] The main purpose of professional instruction in and out of class, according to Quincy, was to drill the student. Anathema indeed to him would have been Dana's former teacher, Mr. Emerson, who later said in his celebrated lecture "Education" that "A rule is so easy that it does not need a man to apply it; an automaton, a machine, can be made to keep a school so."[15]

Feeling like "a slave whipped to his dungeon" (62), Dana returned to Harvard, so well tutored by Woods that drill was now child's play; and, during his sophomore year, he therefore rose in rank from fifteenth to seventh place in his class. He regularly got up his lessons by candlelight before breakfast; and, after meeting his daily duties at school, he devoted his evening hours to unassigned reading. After a pleasant summer vacation at Plymouth, he began his junior year with every expectation of continuing to rise in the academic scale, especially in composition and forensics. But the aftermath of a severe attack of the measles during his Plymouth vacation was weakened eyes which did not respond to treatment. Dana hoped that his eyes would improve;

but, when he found week after week that he could not even look at a printed page without intense pain, he withdrew from college, returned home, and lingered there nearly a year as "a useless, pitied & dissatisfied creature" (63-64).

The miserable fellow was hardly in a position to appreciate the fact then, but his affliction gave him what Bliss Perry has aptly called "Dana's magical chance"[16]—a chance to escape Boston conventionality by going to sea while he was still young. Circumstances dictated his choice, since his father could not afford to send him on a grand tour. Dana could not even have afforded to return to his former tutor Woods at Andover, had his eyes permitted part-time study there. It would have been beneath the dignity of a Dana to head for the Maine woods or for the Adirondacks, or even to camp at some such nearby place as Walden Pond.

But he could go to sea, and he would: "When I recall the motives which governed me in this choice [he later wrote], I can hardly tell which predominated, a desire to cure my eyes, my love of adventure & the attraction of the novelty of a life before the mast, or anxiety to escape from the depressing situation of inactivity & dependence at home" (64-65). So, resolved to go before the mast for the toughening adventure of it all, Dana through the winter and spring sought a berth, and he finally signed aboard the *Pilgrim,* bound for California. She was an eighty-seven-foot brig of one hundred eighty-one tons, which meant that Dana would have plenty of hard work as part of a small crew; and remote California meant a long voyage to a healthy climate. On August 14, 1834, Dana, greener than Walt Whitman's grass, began his poor boy's grand tour. Within a week his Brahmin myopia was gone, and he was as keen-eyed as Keats's stout Cortez, straining to stare at the Pacific Ocean.

CHAPTER 2

Two-Year Log

THE NEXT TWENTY-FIVE months were indeed "Dana's magical chance." By temporarily escaping his Boston Brahmin background, Dana proved that he could stand on his own two feet and be a man. When he left Boston on the *Pilgrim*[1] in August, 1834, he was weak-eyed and unsure of himself, in spite of his valiant attempt to dress the part of a sailor, with loose duck trousers, checked shirt, and tarpaulin hat: ". . . I supposed that I should pass very well for jack tar. But it was impossible to deceive the practised eye in these matters; and while I thought myself to be looking as salt as Neptune himself, I was, no doubt, known for a landsman by every one on board as soon as I hove in sight" (4).* Out of sight of land for the first time, he made friends with Ben Stimson, also young and green, and filled "the perfect silence of the sea" with sweetly melancholy reflections on "the social and intellectual enjoyments of life" (8) now behind him but unforgotten.

Quickly, however, several rudely shouted orders broke in upon his dreams; and the worried looks which the experienced sailors were casting to windward told even him that bad weather was coming as the ship approached the Gulf Stream. Dana was ordered aloft to reef some sails, and he describes the outcome:

> I could not have been of much service, for I remember having been sick several times before I left the topsail yard. Soon all was snug aloft, and we were again allowed to go below. This I did not consider much of a favor, for the confusion of everything below, and that inexpressible sickening smell, caused by the shaking up of bilge-water in the hold,

---

* All parenthetical references in this chapter are to Richard Henry Dana, Jr., *Two Years Before the Mast: A Personal Narrative of Life at Sea*, ed. John Haskell Kemble (Los Angeles, 1964).

made the steerage but an indifferent refuge from the cold,
wet decks. . . . I could not but remember that this was only
the first night of a two years' voyage. (9-10)

But he hung on, boy that he was, and even found it possible
to laugh at himself briefly, like Melville's Wellingborough Redburn. Six days out of Boston, Dana paused after helping to wash
down the decks, swab them, and coil up the rigging; utterly ex-
hausted, he made the mistake of sitting on the spars to await
seven bells for breakfast, with the following result:

> The officer, seeing my lazy posture, ordered me to slush the
> mainmast, from the royal-mast-head, down. The vessel was
> then rolling a little, and I had taken no sustenance for
> three days, so that I felt tempted to tell him that I had rather
> wait till after breakfast; but I knew that I must "take the
> bull by the horns," and that if I showed any sign of want of
> spirit or of backwardness, that I should be ruined at once. So
> I took my bucket of grease and climbed up to the royal-
> mast-head. Here the rocking of the vessel, which increases
> the higher you go from the foot of the mast, which is the
> fulcrum of the lever, and the smell of the grease, which
> offended my fastidious senses, upset my stomach again, and
> I was not a little rejoiced when I got upon the comparative
> terra firma of the deck. (12)

The Negro cook, Thomas Curtis of Boston, then gave Dana
some valuable advice. He told him that now that he had vomited
all his "long-shore *swash*," he should begin a new tack, throw
his sweetmeats overboard, and start gnawing on sea fare. "I cannot describe the change which half a pound of cold salt beef and
a biscuit or two produced in me. I was a new being. . . . When we
went on deck [at noon] I felt somewhat like a man, and could
begin to learn my sea duty with considerable spirit" (12-13).

Two years later, in September, 1836, Dana, then aboard the
Alert on his way back to Boston, was approaching the same Gulf
Stream which had caused his queasiness earlier. This time a lad
came down from the royal-masthead complaining of seasickness,
"caused by the irregular, pitching motion of the vessel, increased
by the height to which he had been above the hull, which is like
the fulcrum of the lever" (336). Another hand went up, but he
became sick also. So the mate, Richard Brown of Marblehead,

who knew a man when he saw one, sent a man up. As we read Dana's words in the next-to-last chapter, we see the contrast with those just quoted from the second chapter:

> The work must be done, and the mate sent me. I did very well for some time, but the pitching overcame me, though I never had been sick since the first two days from Boston, and had been in all sorts of weather and situations. Still, I kept my place, and did not come down, until I had got through my work, which was more than two hours. The ship certainly never acted so badly before. The current and wind running against one another, made such an ugly chopping sea that the vessel was pitched and jerked about in all manner of ways; the sails seeming to have no steadying power over her. The tapering points of the masts made various curves and angles against the sky overhead, and sometimes, in one sweep of an instant, described an arc of more than forty-five degrees, bringing up with a sudden jerk which made it necessary to hold on with both hands, and then sweeping off, in another long, irregular curve. I was not positively sick, and came down with a look of indifference, yet was not unwilling to get upon the comparative terra firma of the deck. (336-37)

Dana had sailed from Boston on the *Pilgrim,* a pilgrim lad in search of freedom and new lands; he returned on the *Alert,* a man alert in mind and body. In his final chapter, immediately after describing his curious indifference about returning home to Boston Harbor, he added that it would take some excitement to rouse him. "And the next morning, when all hands were called, and we were busily at work, clearing the decks, and getting everything in readiness . . . mind and body seemed to wake together" (344).

I *To California*

Dana had spent only 285 days at sea, or a little less than ten months, out of his twenty-five months and eight days as a sailor. Hence the title *Two Years Before the Mast* is inaccurate. For almost sixteen months he was in California, on land or on coastal voyages to various points from San Diego to San Francisco. He had left Boston on August 14, 1834, on the *Pilgrim,* under the command of Captain Francis A. Thompson, about thirty years of age. A day later the brig prepared for sea, and Dana stood his first watch. A day after that the *Pilgrim* went to the lower harbor and at midnight started in earnest for California. By August 20 the men were glad to be past the worst part of the Gulf Stream, and Dana heard for the first time the pleasant sea-cry "Sail ho!" as they sighted two inward-bound American vessels. Within a couple of weeks they had hailed three more ships. On September 7, the *Pilgrim* picked up the welcome northeast trade winds and made fine time for a couple of uneventful weeks. Then on September 22 she was chased by a clipper-built brig showing no colors. The *Pilgrim* outran and lost its piratical pursuer by spreading more canvas, wetting the sails, running dead before the wind, and altering course through the moonless night.

On October 1 the ship crossed the equator on what was logged at long. 24° 24′ W. This figure, which Dana reports but does not explicitly question, was an error, because four days later "Land ho!" alerted him to join the others in making out Recife, then called Pernambuco. Captain Thompson stopped using his faulty chronometer at this point, because by its calculation his brig was in long. 25° W., which is almost 10° east of Recife. Meanwhile, a couple of days before sighting South American land, Captain Thompson was probably edgy because he thought he was far off course. So, when he caught his second mate George Forster of Scituate, Massachusetts, snoozing while on duty, he broke him to common sailor; asked the crew to nominate a replacement; and, when the men by protocol declined, named seaman James Hall of Boston to the post.

Two or three weeks later the *Pilgrim* was due east of the mouth of the river La Plata, which is flanked by Montevideo, Uruguay, and by Buenos Aires, Argentina. Here they encountered their first storm, and Dana had his first chance to witness and be tested by sudden rain, hail, and high winds. During the next week or ten days the *Pilgrim* sailed into ever-higher southern latitudes, and her men readied themselves and the vessel for Cape Horn and its bitter cold. At daybreak on November 4 they saw the two Falkland Islands and, sailing between them and the Patagonian mainland, sighted the Island of Staten Land at sunset. Then they had four days of mixed weather, sometimes pleasant and with fair winds, sometimes squally or worse, with sleet knifing the men and snow covering the deck.

On one of these days Dana first stood his two-hour trick at the helm. "Inexperienced as I was, I made out to steer to the satisfaction of the officer, and neither Stimson nor myself . . . gave up our tricks, all the time that we were off the Cape" (30). On November 8 they stalled in a dead calm and thick fog, which soon turned to hail, snow, and wild winds. The next day, Sunday, started clear, as all the other Sundays since Boston had been. Captain Thompson got an observation of the sun at noon, which was fortunate for a ship off Cape Horn with a useless chronometer.

But in the late afternoon a blinding hailstorm lashed at them out of the southwest. All hands went aloft as the brig plunged into the swelling seas. At one point the mate ordered the spencer-mast jib furled. "This was no agreeable or safe duty, yet it must be done. An old Swede, (the best sailor on board,) . . . sprang out upon the bowsprit. Another one must go: I was near the mate—there was no hanging back—I sprang forward . . . and jumped between the knight-heads out upon the bowsprit" (32). While on the jib-boom, which repeatedly dived into huge waves, Dana and John the Swede furled the jib "and, coming in over the staysail nettings, were not a little pleased to find that all was snug, and the watch gone below; for we were soaked through, and it was very cold" (32).

For the next four days the *Pilgrim* drove on through heavy seas and fierce winds, often through snow and hail. By November 14, the captain reckoned that they were well west of Cape Horn and therefore started bearing north as much as he dared without letting the prevailing southwest winds dash him against the rocky coast of Chile. On the same day the *Pilgrim* sighted a Poughkeepsie whaler, and next day Thompson gammed with her captain, Job Terry. Straightened out as to his longitude, Thompson altered course to the north and made for Robinson Crusoe's island of Juan Fernandez, to bookish Dana's delight.

On November 17, the call "All hands ahoy! a man overboard!" startled Dana and his watch from their early morning sleep. George Ballmer, identified as "an English lad who was the life of the crew" (33), had been climbing aloft to strap a masthead for halyards when, with the strap and block and also a coil of rope and a spike hanging around his neck, he fell from the shrouds into the water, evidently sank at once, and was never seen again. A quarter-boat was lowered and pulled about for an hour, but to no avail. Dana had now been touched by death at sea—that "speechlessly quick chaotic bundling of a man into Eternity," as we read of it in *Moby Dick*.[2]

On November 25, the island of Juan Fernandez loomed ahead, and a day later Dana went ashore with the water detail and thus was allowed to set foot on land again for the first time since leaving home 104 days before. He improved his limited free time by observing the convict labor gangs, the topography of the islands, their fish, and even Captain Thompson's dinner guests aboard ship. It was well that Dana was allowed his island respite because, from November 27 until California forty-seven days later, he saw neither land nor other ship.

The *Pilgrim* next caught the southeast trade winds and had three weeks of easy sailing, during which the men were ordered to get the ship into trim for coastal service as both trader and hide-hauler. For Dana, this work meant being introduced to the refinements of setting the rigging taut, rattling the lower rigging, tarring down all standing-rigging, and painting the entire ship inside and out and down to the water's edge. On December 19 they crossed the equator again. Within a week the crew was permitted to celebrate Christ's birth with plum duff and molasses for dinner.

About this time Dana and Stimson petitioned the captain for permission to shift their berths from steerage to forecastle.

> This, to our delight, was granted, and we turned in to *bunk* and mess with the crew forward. We now began to feel like sailors, which we never fully did when we were in the steerage. While there, however useful and active you may be, you are but a mongrel . . . You are immediately under the eye of the officers, cannot dance, sing, play, smoke, make a noise, or *growl*, (i.e., complain,) or take any other sailor's pleasure . . . But if you live in the forecastle, you are . . . a *sailor*. You hear sailor's talk, learn their ways, their peculiarities of feeling as well as speaking and acting; and moreover pick up a great deal of curious and useful information in seamanship, ship's customs, foreign countries, &c., from their long yarns and equally long disputes. No man can be a sailor, or know what sailors are, unless he has lived in the forecastle with them—turned in and out with them, eaten of their dish and drank of their cup. (52, 54)

After much evidence of the continuing irritability of the captain, the *Pilgrim* reached the latitude of Point Conception, due west of Santa Barbara and a little north of the present city of Los Angeles. They swung east and sailed thus for several days. On January 13, 1835, they made land at Point Conception, and a day later they cast anchor in the bay of Santa Barbara—150 days from Boston. The green lad had proved himself a man at sea. He would now have a chance to show his worth ashore.

II *In California*

His sixteen months on and just off the coast of California were more varied and hence more educative to Dana than his five months at sea had been. But, at the same time, California was less a test of his manhood than Cape Horn had been and would be again on the homeward journey. Therefore, though one must recognize the value of *Two Years Before the Mast* as a source book of early Californiana, its twenty chapters devoted to Dana's experiences at San Diego, San Juan, Catalina Island, San Pedro, Los Angeles, San Buenaventura, Santa Barbara, Point Conception, Carmel, Piños, Monterey, Año Nuevo, and San Francisco are less thrilling to most readers.

The *Pilgrim* first put in at Santa Barbara, the central port of the entire coast which the company wished to work; and she awaited the arrival of the company agent, Alfred Robinson. January being the middle of the November-to-April rainy season in California, the brig lay at anchor three miles from shore with slip-ropes on her cables, ready to seek the safety of the sea in the event of a sudden storm. The first boat ashore on January 14 landed Captain Thompson. In the second boat, the one ordered ashore at sundown to pick him up, was Dana: "I shall never forget the impression which our first attempt at landing on the beach of California made upon me. The sun had just gone down; it was getting dusky; the damp night wind was beginning to blow, and the heavy swell of the Pacific was setting in, and breaking in loud and high 'combers' upon the beach" (61).

Dana and his mates were novices at handling rowboats in a California surf. So they lay on their oars and watched until the Hawaiian crew off the *Ayacucho*, an Ecuador-built brig also trading in California, ran its boat up on the sand high and dry.

Then the *Pilgrim* crew did the same. Finding that Captain Thompson was not yet ready to be pulled back to his ship, Dana and most of the others took advantage of their leisure by walking on the smooth sand, watching the long waves sweep in and break, observing the Sandwich Islanders load their piles of bullock hides and bags of tallow, and admiring their method of getting their laden boat well off and out of the breakers on its way to the *Ayacucho.* Dana missed nothing: "The sand of the beach began to be cold to our bare feet; the frogs set up their croaking in the marshes, and one solitary owl, from the end of the distant point, gave out his melancholy note, mellowed by the distance, and we began to think that it was high time for 'the old man' . . . to come down" (64). In a short while he came, and they shoved off for the *Pilgrim* again.

Thus began Dana's tour of duty in California. The weather that night produced a sudden storm, which obliged Captain Thompson to follow the *Ayacucho's* lead—slip cables and seek open water. Back again to Santa Barbara the next day, the ship picked up some passengers, including the agent of the company, and Captain Thompson's brother and his wife. That night the *Pilgrim* set sail for Monterey. Dana's California adventures had begun.

The next four months were a monotonous succession of coastal voyages for the purposes of loading hides and tallow and of trading items of cargo brought from Boston. Those months were notable for little but intensely hard work and very little free time. At Monterey in mid-January, 1835, five Mexican customs inspectors boarded the *Pilgrim* to examine her cargo and manifest; and the next day began a week or ten days of rowing potential customers between the shore and the ship-turned-store: "Our cargo was an assorted one; that is, it consisted of everything under the sun" (82). Dana considered the native Californians to be both lazy and stupid; he thought them foolish for buying bad Boston wine and for trading two hides for one pair of shoes. He observed that the company markup was about 300 per cent on Boston prices.

When trade began to slacken at Monterey, the *Pilgrim* saluted the Presidio there and set sail for Santa Barbara again, where for two weeks the crew landed goods and began the arduous business of loading hides. The men were dismayed to learn that their ship was to collect forty thousand hides for the ship *California* and in addition load their own *Pilgrim* with twelve to fifteen thousand more. At first they had planned to be on the uncivilized coast a year or two at most; now the rumor sprang up that they might be there for three years at least. Under the pressure of this fear, the Brahmin in Dana came to the fore. In his worried imagination, three years stretched to four, and he became deeply depressed, feeling that he would have to be a sailor for life.

Other troubles developed. They lost nearly a week during a rainy southeaster off Santa Barbara. Then they picked up another officer, Mr. Russell by name—"a short, red-haired, round-shouldered, vulgar-looking fellow, who had lost one eye, and squinted with the other" (97-98). He was hardly a working replacement for poor drowned George Ballmer or another mate, Henry Mellus, now rheumatic and converted to a clerk. Next, the *Pilgrim* coasted down from Santa Barbara to the town of Los Angeles and San Pedro, its port, where the men landed forty tons of goods and took on about two thousand hides.

Worse than storms, an ugly new officer, a diminished crew, or backbreaking work was Captain Thompson, who now got thoroughly out of humor. It had been coming for some time. His mate, Andrew B. Amerzene, was too good-natured and easygoing: "a more honest, upright, and kind-hearted man I never saw," Dana explained, adding however, in criticism, "He was not the man to call a sailor a 'son of a b——h,' and knock him down with a handspike. He wanted the energy and spirit for such a voyage as ours, and for such a captain" (96). Seemingly, when the mate is too soft, the captain becomes too hard; or so it happened on the *Pilgrim*.

One day Captain Thompson got into a scuffle with a sailor he mistakenly regarded as lazy and sullen, Samuel Sparks of Virginia. He had a speech impediment,[3] was slow of movement, was not very able, but seemed always to do as well as he could. Sam had hurt his hand shifting goods in the hold and, beginning to stammer out an oath or two, was overheard by the captain, who roughly demanded an explanation. In pain, Sam stuttered a brief reply, whereupon Thompson hit him and soon got him down. When the captain ordered him to give him no more "jaw," Sam was man enough to reply, "I never gave you any, sir" (103). The result was a flogging which sickened Dana—a flogging not only of the innocent stammerer but also of one of his shipmates, John the Swede, who had dared to ask his captain why he was going to flog Sam.

Frank Thompson showed his true colors. He hit poor Sam a dozen or more times with a thick rope end. Then he did the same for John Linden. Dancing with sadistic pleasure, Thompson shouted, "If you want to know what I flog you for, I'll tell you. It's because I like to do it!—because I like to do it! It suits me! That's what I do it for!" (104) When his victim writhed out an appeal to Christ, the wild captain shouted, *"Call on Frank Thompson!* He's the man! He can help you! Jesus Christ can't help you now!"* (105). The whole graphic scene, one of the most memorable in the book, is reminiscent of one in Melville's *White-Jacket,* in which sadistic Captain Claret, flogging four of his men, tells the last and youngest, "I would not forgive God Almighty!"[4]

Dana responded to the flogging in several ways. First, he turned away and evidently vomited over the rail. Next, he quickly concluded that the captain would not attempt to lay a hand on him. Then he vowed that he would "do something to redress the grievances and relieve the sufferings of that poor class of beings, of whom [he] was then one" (106). And finally, he closely observed the reactions of the two victims and indeed of the whole crew for weeks afterwards, noting that John was mainly angered by the physical affront and talked irresponsibly of revenge, that Sam felt degraded and lost his cheerful elasticity and wanted only to have the accursed voyage done with, and that the crew grew sullen and refused to sing at work or get away from San Pedro for San Diego with a will. Not checking Dana's text, D. H. Lawrence has some typically Lawrencian fun at poor Sam's expense:

> And whack! Whack! down on the bare back of that sloucher Sam comes the cat.
> What does it do? By Jove, it goes like ice-cold water into his spine. Down those lashes runs the current of the Captain's rage, right into the blood and into the toneless ganglia of Sam's voluntary system. Crash! Crash! runs the lightning flame, right into the cores of the living nerves.
> And the living nerves respond. They start to vibrate. They brace up. The blood begins to go quicker. The nerves begin

to recover their vividness. It is their tonic. The man Sam has a new clear day of intelligence, and a smarty back. The Captain has a new relief, a new ease in his authority, and a sore heart.

There is a new equilibrium, and a fresh start. The *physical* intelligence of a Sam is restored, the turgidity is relieved from the veins of the Captain.

It is a natural form of human coition, interchange.

It is good for Sam to be flogged. It is good, on this occasion, for the Captain to have Sam flogged. I say so. Because they were both in that physical condition.[5]

However, Dana's physical and intellectual responses are more to the point than Lawrence's.

By March 14 the *Pilgrim* had passed San Juan and cast anchor in the little harbor of San Diego, but not before Captain Thompson had smashed his vessel into the *Lagoda*, a rusty-looking hide-drogher in the San Diego channel. While backing and filling, Thompson's ship then drifted into the *Loriotte*, a trader from Genoa. Next beginning to drift toward the *Ayacucho*, Captain Thompson suffered the embarrassment of having to be rescued by Captain John Wilson of the *Ayacucho*, who came aboard the *Pilgrim* and "in an easy, fatherly kind of way" (112-14) countermanded Thompson's inept orders, got the ship disentangled, and anchored her abreast of the company hide-house. Dana and his mates were silently delighted, and more so when Captain Bradshaw of the *Lagoda* answered the report that Captain Thompson had come aboard for a visit by bawling out from the companionway, "Has he brought his brig with him?" (114).

After an almost unique liberty Sunday in San Diego and its environs, a week followed which was full of hard work landing hides and preparing the ship for more. Forster, the former second mate now broken to common seaman, deserted and made good his escape by concealing himself in the nearby hide-house of the *Lagoda*, which he ultimately signed aboard. On March 27 the *Pilgrim* sailed to San Pedro for more hides, and then returned to Santa Barbara in mid-April. The following Sunday, which was Easter, Dana was permitted "to go ashore and misspend" (133), as he rather puritanically put it, a rare, free Sabbath. After two more weeks of hide collecting, the *Pilgrim* went back to San Pedro.

Then, early in May, the *Pilgrim* coasted down to San Juan. The *Lagoda* crew reported this hilly, rocky, and exposed place to be the worst on the entire coast; but to Dana it was "the only romantic spot in California" (141). At the first opportunity, while awaiting the return of Robinson, the agent who was on business at the Mission of San Juan Capistrano, Dana thoroughly explored the cliffs. He found shells, watched the sea tumble among the crevices of rocks, compared the rocks to those of Nahant and Newport, and—in short—invited his soul:

> I separated myself from the rest, and sat down on a rock . . . Compared with the plain, dull sand-beach of the rest of the coast, this grandeur was as refreshing as a great rock in a weary land. It was almost the first time that I had been positively alone . . . since I had left home. My better nature returned strong upon me. Everything was in accordance with my state of feeling, and I experienced a glow of pleasure at finding that the little poetry and romance I ever had in me, had not been entirely deadened by the laborious and frittering life I had led, but could be revived by a strong action of concurrent outward things. Nearly an hour did I sit, almost lost in the luxury of this entire new scene of the play in which I had been so long acting, when I was aroused by the distant shouts of my companions . . . (142)[6]

The interlude was soon over; but the spot is now called Dana Point, and is in Orange County, California.

On May 8, 1835, the *Pilgrim* returned to San Diego, and an entirely new phase began for Dana. He was ordered to join the work gang at the hide-house. There, for the next four months he and six others cured hides under the solitary eye of the hated Russell. Dana's companions were Samuel Hooper, Jr., a twelve-year-old boy from Marblehead; a huge but gentle Frenchman named Nicholas, "of a frame so large that he might have been shown for a curiosity" (147); and four Hawaiians from a colony of contentedly unemployed fellows living in an abandoned oven built by some Russian explorers on the beach. As usual, Dana made good use of his free time by learning what Nicholas could teach him; and, in gratitude for a sympathetic ear, the giant combined forces with Dana to hold Russell in awe. Dana also studied the language, habits, and nature of his new Hawaiian friends, whom he ultimately came to respect highly.

Dana soon mastered the details of hide-curing. The whole process was yet another test of endurance. A hundred and fifty hides were tied down on the bench and left for the tide to soak. Two days later they were taken by wheelbarrow to vats of strong brine and pickled for two more days. Next they were put on a platform to dry for a day, and then they were spread on the ground, stretched, and staked out skin up to dry. While still drying in the morning, they were knelt on and all corruptible and rough parts were cut away to insure pure and close stowage later. Then the stakes were drawn, and the hides were doubled hair out to dry. The next day they were opened again more thoroughly; that night they were thrown on a horizontal pole and flailed free of dust. Finally they were stowed in the hide-house —a large building of rough boards designed to hold forty thousand hides, and fitted out with a corner as a dirt-floor dormitory for the workers and with an attic room for Russell "the grand."

By soaking a hundred and fifty hides on the beach each day, the six workers had the same number at every stage of curing at all times; at the end of each day during the six-day work week, each person had finished twenty-five hides. The men worked hard and became experts. Soon they learned to have three hours to themselves every afternoon before beating and stowing the dry hides. Their evenings were completely free. On Sundays they were idle unless they chose to kill and dress their weekly bullock. A couple of afternoons a week they conducted wood-gathering expeditions in the nearby hilly bush.

Their somewhat monotonous routine was occasionally broken by the cry "Sail ho!" Sometimes this meant that a native woman was to be seen walking by from town, or perhaps only an ox drawing a cart. But once it actually signaled the arrival of two ships, the *Rosa* and the *Catalina*. Dana had seen the *Rosa*, a large Genoese ship with a high poop, on his first day ashore at Santa Barbara. The *Catalina* was the same brig which had disappointed Dana and his mates just after Easter, when she had entered the Santa Barbara harbor flying an American flag; hoping for news from home, the *Pilgrim* had prepared to welcome a curiously dusky boat crew aboard. But the *Catalina* had proved to be from Oahu, and hence the only things Yankee about her were her captain, officers, papers, and colors.

When the *Rosa* and the *Catalina* crews visited Dana and his cronies at San Diego, they were exceedingly welcome. The hide-house became a genuine melting pot, and Dana must have learned much which Harvard never taught him. One wishes that he had told us more than simply this about the assembly:

> We had now, out of forty or fifty [men], representatives from almost every nation under the sun: two Englishmen, three Yankees, two Scotchmen, two Welshmen, one Irishman, three Frenchmen (two of whom were Normans, and the third from Gascony), one Dutchman, one Austrian, two or three Spaniards, (from old Spain), half a dozen Spanish-Americans and half-breeds, two native Indians from Chili [*sic*] and the Island of Chiloe, one Negro, one Mulatto, about twenty Italians, from all parts of Italy, as many more Sandwich-Islanders [Hawaiians], one Otheitan [Tahitian], and one Kanaka from the Marquesas Islands. (160)

Dana tells us only that they sang various national songs, drank and exchanged stories and advice, and borrowed on another's books.

By late June, Dana and his mates had processed all the hides available and had little to do but await the return of the wandering *Pilgrim*, which arrived again on July 8 with a new captain, Edward H. Faucon, and with a bundle of clothes and eleven letters for Dana from Boston shipped via the *Alert*, now commanded by Captain Thompson. Three days later, with his letters from home memorized and a fresh supply of hides waiting, Dana returned to his routine at the hide-house. By August 1, he and his mates had finished curing all the hides and were obliged to tackle the horrible chore of cleaning out the vats—"in which . . . work we spent two days, up to our knees in mud and the sediments of six months' hide-curing, in a stench which would drive an Irishman from his breakfast" (174). For the next three or more weeks Dana was free to ready his gear and himself for a transfer to the *Alert*, which arrived on August 25.

Dana wanted to sign at once aboard this fast Indiaman, operated by the same company as the *Pilgrim* was; for he knew that she would be in Boston a year or two ahead of the *Pilgrim*, which was destined to ply the California coast gathering hides for other ships, including the *Alert*. Further, his packet of letters from home had told Dana that, at the request of his Boston friends, the owners had ordered Captain Thompson to take him aboard; and Dana wanted to see the order carried out immediately. So he made formal application to the hated officer:

> He told me that I could go home in the ship when she sailed (which I knew before); and, finding that I wished to be on board while she was on the coast, said he had no objection, if I could find one of my own age to exchange with me, for the time. This, I easily accomplished, for they were glad to change the scene by a few months on shore, and moreover, escape the winter and the south-easters.
>
> . . . By night I got my chest, hammock, clothes, and everything in order, and found myself once more afloat, and before the mast in a big ship. (178)

The situation is somewhat equivocal. One wonders whether Dana told his replacement ashore that coastal duty for him might last two more years. Dana does not say, nor did he mention this touchy subject when he explained matters concerning his transfer in a letter to his father from Monterey: "My reasons for doing this were that a large and fine ship like the *Alert* is a more comfortable vessel than a small brig; and that her duty on the coast is pleasanter. Also the customs and style of seamanship are different and superior on board a large vessel; and I wished to become acquainted with the ship's company with whom I was to make the voyage."[7]

Dana seems to have convinced himself that an exchange "for the time" might be long enough to include "the voyage home." At any rate, on September 8, 1835, he took up his duties aboard the *Alert* in San Diego Harbor and thus began the second leg of his grand adventure.

He immediately began getting acquainted with the *Alert*, which was newer and bigger than the old *Pilgrim*, and more than twice as heavy. Being so much grander, she normally carried a crew of five or six more than that of the *Pilgrim*, which in addition had now been lightened by death, sickness, and desertion.[8] Dana soon settled into life aboard the *Alert*, made friends with several of her old hands, and developed such pride in the new vessel that he quickly identified with her rather self-consciously and became critical of the discredited old *Pilgrim*, with which the *Alert* rendezvoused at San Pedro to take off her cargo.

"These hides made but little show in our hold, though they had loaded the *Pilgrim* down to the water's edge. . . . The *Pilgrim's* crew envied me my place on board the ship, and seemed to think that I had got a little windward of them; especially in the matter of going home first" (186-87). And well they might: few of them had influential friends back in Boston.

For three weeks the *Alert* lay at San Pedro landing cargo and loading more hides; then she raced the *Catalina* to Santa Barbara. By mid-October, the *Alert* was at San Diego again, and on October 20 back at San Juan, where Dana had romantically mused at the lonely point six months before. This time, perhaps to impress the *Alert* crew, probably also to ingratiate himself with Captain Thompson, but mostly to meet a new challenge, Dana volunteered to be lowered by rope from the rocky precipice to dislodge a dozen or twenty hides caught in the rocks halfway down from the heights off which they had been hurled during loading. Then the ship sailed through a storm to San Pedro; on November 1, they worked out of the harbor to set sail for Santa Barbara.

The next month was divided between routine duty at that port and herculean work at sea: a five-day gale caught the ship part way up to Monterey and blew her off course half the distance to Hawaii; then she had to make sail slowly and beat to windward to San Francisco, where she arrived on December 4 only to be pinned down by three weeks of rain. The men visited a Russian brig from Sitka and unloaded hide-launches manned by Indians. Dana once joined a wood-gathering gang on an unpleasant three-day expedition to Angel Island in the northern part of San Francisco Bay. But he thus avoided the even worse duty of the water party ordered to fill all the ship's casks or of the hide-loaders at San Jose and Santa Clara. Two days after Christmas, the *Alert* unmoored for Monterey, where Captain Faucon of the *Pilgrim* was anxiously awaiting her and fearful that she had been lost.

On January 6, 1836, the *Alert* sailed with some Mexican passengers bound for Santa Barbara; but life was not simply a matter of casting anchor, rowing passengers ashore, and slipping cables to ride out storms at sea: Dana and a few of his cronies were permitted to observe some of the festivities surrounding the marriage of company-agent Robinson to a daughter of the important Guerra family of California. On February 1 the *Alert* left for San Pedro, there meeting the *Pilgrim,* which the crew had not seen for nearly five months. Emotional though Dana was at seeing the *Pilgrim* again, there was not much time for reminiscing or for chatting with his former shipmates: on February 6 the *Alert* was at San Diego. Dana at once went to the old Russian oven to spend an evening with his Hawaiian friends, including a lad named Hope, then languishing under the white man's burden of venereal disease. Refused by Captain Thompson, Dana went ahead and got some calomel for the boy from Richard Brown, the admirable mate of the *Alert.*

Another diversion at this time was the downfall of the one-eyed hide-house master, Russell, who was evidently a disreputable man. Dana loathed him and poured some of his relatively rare sarcasm into one description of him in his attic room at the hide-house: "There he lived in solitary grandeur: eating and sleeping alone, (and these were his principal occupations,) and communing with his own dignity" (147). He was not always alone, however: he was suspected of wasting his men's provisions of tea, flour, and sugar in the town of San Diego; and he was observed treating squaws to stores of molasses on the beach. So the men were probably happy when he was fired for his misdeeds, became a hunted desperado, turned up back at the hide-house begging for food and shelter, and finally gave himself up and was dragged off to jail.

The *Alert* returned to San Pedro on February 13, casting anchor just in time to slip again and seek shelter off Catalina Island during a three-day northeaster. A week later the *California* arrived from Boston and dropped a packet of letters and newspapers for the men of the *Alert.* A couple of days later they left "this rascally hole of San Pedro" (247) for Santa Barbara. Unable to gam with the *California,* Dana and his shipmates had to rely for news on a file of Boston papers which Captain Thompson read and then handed down to them.

March 5 was the beginning of a change. Captain Thompson was observed shaking hands with his friends on the beach of Santa Barbara. Dana bid farewell forever to his new friend George Marsh, an English sailor whose life at sea had been varied and exciting and who was transferred from seaman on the *Alert* to second mate on Captain Wilson's *Ayacucho*—with, incidentally, no apparent objection from testy Thompson. The *Alert* passed hated San Pedro and then the romantic cliff near San Juan, and on March 10 anchored for the last time at San Diego, where her crew faced the arduous two-month task of emptying and fumigating her and stuffing her full of forty thousand hides and other goods.

First the crew dumped ballast, by rowing it to the point when Presidio inspection personnel were aboard but otherwise by illegally if efficiently tubbing it overboard. Then the men broke the Sabbath by smoking the *Alert*—starting a slow fire of charcoal, bark, and sulfur on ballast in the hold, and then calking all hatches and open seams, and pasting shut the windows and scuttle-slides and any cracks where wisps of acrid smoke crept out. When she was pure again, her crew jammed her with hides, "from the grey of the morning till star-light, for six weeks, with the exception of Sundays, and of just time to swallow our meals" (254).

The work was divided into specialties: some men threw the hides out of the house, some hung them on horizontal poles, some flailed the accumulated dust out of them, and some piled them on a platform; gangs of other men filed to the water with hides on their heads and sloshed to waiting boats, which still others pulled to the ship off shore. Meanwhile the older men, whom the nippingly cold water might have made sick, were busy stowing the hides by an ingenious process called "steeving."

To "steeve," they first leveled the ballast just above the keelson and covered it with dunnage. Then they carefully built up layer upon layer of hides to within four feet of the beams. Next they took "twenty-five to fifty hides, doubled at the backs, and put into one another, like the leaves of a book" (256). Making an opening between two piled hides, they inserted the spine, so to speak, of the "book," and then placed smooth, greased strips of wood over and under it. Two long sharpened wedges of wood were inserted through the center of the "book" to press inside against its back. Finally, by means of blocks and tackles pushing on the exposed ends of the wedges, rather like slow bowstrings on slow arrows, the men jammed a hundred and fifty hides into a pile to which the strongest hand could not have added a single hide.

To pull in unison, the men were cheered on by various nautical

46

songs. Dana notes that certain songs worked better than others: " 'Heave round hearty!' 'Capt'n gone ashore!' and the like, might do for common pulls, but on an emergency, when we wanted a heavy, 'raise-the-dead' pull, which should start the beams of the ship, there was nothing like 'Time for us to go!' 'Grog time a day,' 'Hurrah! hurrah! my hearty bullies!' or 'Round the corner, Sally!' " (257).

April 15 brought the *Pilgrim*, commanded by Faucon, who released Dana's old friend Stimson to the *Alert* in exchange for one Tom Harris. Dana was delighted to have Stimson beside him again, but he hated to say goodbye to Harris, long his companion in the anchor watch on the *Alert* and a knowledgeable shipmate. Like George Marsh, Harris was lured away by the promise of an officer's berth. Then on April 24 the *California* arrived with agent Robinson aboard. After the crew of the *California* had unloaded her hides, some of her men boarded the *Alert* to help with the final steeving there and shortened the time of doing it by bringing in a fresh repertory of songs.

Then came the worst moment Dana was to know in all his sixteen months on the California coast. Hauled up before Captain Thompson, with both Captain Faucon and Mr. Robinson looking on, he was told to his surprise that he could remain aboard the *Alert* for the return trip to Boston only if he found someone to report in his place on the *Pilgrim*. When he put on his best Brahmin front and reminded Captain Thompson of his orders and his promise, that brawny man pointed out Dana's name on the *Pilgrim's* shipping papers, told him that a captain's power over all crew members was absolute, and ordered him to be silent. Nonetheless, as Dana reports it,

> I repeated what I had said, and insisted upon my right to return in the ship. . . . But it would have all availed me nothing, had I been "some poor body," before this absolute, domineering tribunal who cared as little for the happiness and rights of their slaves, as they did for the precepts of the moral law. But they saw that I would not go, unless "vi et armis," and they knew that, 'though they feared neither God nor regarded man where they were, yet that I had friends and interest enough at home to make them suffer for any injustice they might do me. (261)

Thompson weakened and authorized Dana to pay a sailor thirty dollars to exchange places with him, as Stimson had paid Tom Harris. Can we believe what Dana reports next? "I told him that if any one was sent on board the brig, I should pity him, and be willing to help him to that, or almost any amount; but would not speak of it as an exchange" (261-62).

When Captain Thompson told English Ben, certainly no friend of Boston Brahmins, to take Dana's place for thirty dollars and a suit of clothes, the crew rightly turned on Dana and called him "a gentleman's son" (262). His conscience began to bother him: "The notion that I was not 'one of them,' which, by a participation in all their labor and hardships, and having no favor shown me, had been laid asleep, was beginning to revive. But far stronger than any feeling for myself, was the pity I felt for the poor lad" (262).

Dana still continued to feel, however, that his case was special, that an additional year or two in California would be uniquely harmful to him; yet he wanted to be nominally just to everyone, including himself. So he bought another replacement, young Harry R. May, called "Harry Bluff," for six months' wages and all Dana's spare clothes and books, and thus freed Ben. It is to be doubted that the crew felt more fraternal toward a Brahmin who could buy his way home for half a year's pay; however, company officials impliedly censured Captain Thompson by refunding Dana his wages later in Boston on the grounds that he had signed them away "under compulsion" (263).

During his last few days in California, Dana had charge of some Indians filling water casks for the *Alert*. Then on May 8, dangerously loaded with forty thousand hides, thirty thousand horns, several barrels of otter and beaver skins, numerous spare spars, a colony of livestock, and even a little California gold, the sluggish *Alert* moved slowly out of San Diego Harbor and promptly stuck fast on a sand bar across its mouth. The wind soon backed her into the stream, and at high tide out she went, doomed to wallow in a waterlogged fashion until she could work herself loose. "When all sail had been set, and the decks cleared up, the California was a speck in the horizon, and the coast lay like a low cloud along the north-east. At sunset they were both out of sight, and we were once more upon the ocean, where sky and water meet" (270).

To what in California was Dana bidding farewell until his return twenty-four years later? To months of arduous and monotonous labor, of course, as a willing hand before the masts of the *Pilgrim* and the *Alert,* and ashore loading, unloading, curing, and again loading hides, and following many other orders. But in addition, Dana had been educated in a variety of ways. While still aboard the *Pilgrim* bound for California, he had studied Spanish, and by the time he landed there he was more proficient in the language than anyone else in the crew. So he became the linguist:

> I was often sent for something which I could not tell the name of to save my life; but I liked the business, and accordingly never pleaded ignorance. Sometimes I managed to jump below and take a look at my [borrowed] dictionary before going ashore; or else I overhauled some English resident on my way, and got the word from him; and then by signs, and the help of my Latin and French, contrived to get along. This was a good exercise for me, and no doubt taught me more than I should have learned by months of study and reading; it also gave me opportunities of seeing the customs, characters, and domestic arrangements of the people; beside being a great relief from the monotony of a day spent on board ship. (85)

Also he visited or at least saw the missions of Carmel, Dolores, San Diego, San Gabriel, San Jose, San Juan, San Juan Capistrano, San Luis Obispo, Santa Barbara, Santa Buenaventura, and Santa Clara, and the Presidios of Monterey, San Diego, San Francisco, and Santa Barbara. He saw weddings and funerals, sampled the wares of local *pulperias,* watched native horse races and cockfights and fandangos, and gammed with the motley crews of a dozen ships trading up and down California—the *Ayacucho,* the *California,* the Hawaiian *Diana* from the northwest coast, the Mexican *Fazio* which had run ashore at San Pedro, the *Lagoda,* the *Loriotte,* the *Rosa,* and others. He listened to Spanish music and the curious Hawaiian sea-cries and improvised gutteral songs, and to various foreign tongues, from pure Castilian to the slobbering grunts of half-breeds.

He coldly judged every person he met or saw, judged him by his own high standards and measured him against himself as to breeding, education, and ability to make use of opportunities presented by fate. He admired most the high-born Spanish-Californian aristocrats and the innately decent Sandwich Islanders, and he admired least the greasily commercial Yankees whom the bait of high profits had lured to California.

III Back from California

The return to Boston of the *Alert* took fifteen days less time than the outward-bound voyage to California of the *Pilgrim*. This was because, in spite of the unbelievably difficult time the *Alert* had in rounding Cape Horn in midwinter, she bowled along at other times, once making twelve hundred miles south of the equator in a week. And later, once past the Horn and up into fine weather again, they covered two thousand miles in a nine-day period.

But between these two accomplishments the *Alert* had to double the Cape, an epic event which Dana magnificently describes. Almost from the time they left California, the crew members were busy preparing the ship and themselves for the ordeal. They set up the rigging and made all sails ready; they overhauled their wretched wardrobes and even painted some of their garments to waterproof them; and one afternoon they made a regular laundry by stopping the scuppers and filling the decks while Captain Thompson conveniently napped below. Toward the end of May, on the 28th, Dana crossed the equator for the third time, and the breezes continued fine. May yielded to June, and the *Alert*, thoroughly loose now, had increased her speed by a third since sluggishly leaving San Diego. Late in June, at about lat. 35° S., the days grew shorter, the sun ran lower and lower, and the nights became cold. On June 26 Captain Thompson reckoned his position at lat. 47° 50′ S., long. 113° 49′ W., and Dana privately calculated Cape Horn to be eighteen hundred miles away. Again the good captain was seemingly highly inaccurate, or else he was timidly steering a full twenty degrees farther west than was necessary. On July 1 Dana estimated that they had forty degrees of easting to make, and they braced themselves to hit the Cape within ten days.

To make matters worse, Dana soon began suffering from a violent toothache, which almost doubled the size of his face and made it impossible for him to open his mouth to eat. When the kind steward asked the captain for rice to boil for Dana, the answer was cold profanity; however, Mr. Brown smuggled some rice into the galley for the cook to boil secretly. At the same time that he reluctantly obeyed the mate's order to rest below, the ship, now about twenty degrees west of the Horn, began to run into large fields of floating ice occasionally punctuated by dangerous islands of ice hundreds of feet high. Once, the captain posted his men on an eighteen-hour watch to guide the ship around the ice islands.

The next day the captain continued hove-to so long, in spite of a breeze, that the men began to talk of mutiny, which, when Mr. Brown reported it to him, he treated with unpredictable mildness. For two more days Dana continued sick, and the ship remained ice-locked; rumors had it that Captain Thompson would put into Valparaiso to winter there, then that he was going to wriggle out of the ice and return home by way of South Africa. But the men were at last ordered to overhaul the deep-sea lead-line and ground-tackles, which meant that they were going to try running the tricky Straits of Magellan just north of Cape Horn. By this time Dana, who had been sick from about July 6 to July 9, was doing his share of the heavy work again. On July 10 and July 11 the ship edged laboriously toward the mouth of the Straits, only to run into impossible gale winds and a solid wall of ice.

So the *Alert* headed due south to try again to double the Cape. This time, being south of the Straits of Magellan, the ship was less than five hundred miles from Cape Horn and therefore all were hopeful of being free of ice. But suddenly islands of ice seemed to jump from the sea and crawl threateningly about the ship. Next, the fiercest storm they had yet experienced crashed upon them from dead ahead. For eight days they drifted helplessly; then, when the wind shifted a little south, they braced to make some headway. But the next night it blew even worse, with hail and snow, and the mainsail slatting like thunder. Then for two days they took advantage of fairly steady south winds, which on July 22 turned briefly into another gale. That afternoon Dana was below with the third mate at the bread locker when warm sunshine suddenly bathed the companionway and shouts volleyed from the deck. When the officer hailed him, the steward in the pantry replied, "Lan' o, to be sure, sir! No you hear 'em sing out, 'Lan' o?' De cap'em say 'im Cape Horn!" (312).

The land was the Island of Staten Land, which the *Alert's* only passenger, a naturalist named Professor Thomas Nuttall from Harvard College, said he would like to go ashore to explore. Bidding him go to hell instead, Captain Thompson resolutely pressed on into the Atlantic Ocean. Putting on every thread of canvas possible, and then a little more, to take advantage of a booming wind from the southwest, the captain headed the ship straight north and ran well inside the Falkland Islands. By July 24 she was in lat. 50° S., past the islands; a week later she was nearly in the latitude of Buenos Aires, and a week after that almost to that of Rio de Janeiro though east of that city by more than fifteen degrees.

At about this time three events provided Dana and the others with some diversion. The captain, though nominally in command of everything aboard, ventured to leave his traditional position aft and wander into Mr. Brown's realm forward. Hot words followed, to the delight of the crew; but the matter was soon undramatically settled in private. Next the steward refused to get Mr. Brown a glass of water, saying loftily that he waited only on the captain. The steward had custom on his side but forgot to call Brown "Mr. Brown." Soon the two were hard at it, wrestling and rolling about. Just as the steward shouted that blood would be spilled, the captain chanced to come on deck and, hearing the veiled threat, seized the steward and flogged him. Significantly, Dana records not one word of criticism at this beating. Then, on the same day, Dana was working aloft on the topgallant yard ninety or more feet above the deck. The yard had been hoisted up and was hanging by a tie. Just after Dana had grasped the rigging, finished with an hour's work, and was taking his second foot off the yard, the tie broke and dropped the yard from under him. He was safe in the rigging; but, if the tie had parted an instant sooner, he would have been pitched overboard or smashed to death on the deck.

On August 12 the *Alert* sighted the island of Trinidad; six days later, Fernando Naronha, not far off the eastern tip of Brazil. A day after that Dana crossed the equator for the fourth time. The *Alert* had journeyed more than four thousand somewhat indirect miles from the Island of Staten Land in twenty-seven efficient days. Early in September they "lay 'humbugging about' in the Horse latitudes, with all sorts of winds and weather, and occasionally, as we were in the latitude of the West Indies,—a thunder storm" (327).

When the trade winds deserted the ship due east of Cuba, she ran into a calm so dead that the mate eerily whispered his orders and the captain fell moodily silent. Suddenly a corposant began to wander on the main topgallant masthead, then disappeared only to show itself again elsewhere. Rain began to patter, thunder grumbled, lightning flashed, and a little wind puffed, "and all was as still as ever" (329). And then,

> A moment more, and a terrific peal and flash came simultaneously upon us, and a cloud appeared to open directly over our heads and let down the water in one body, like a falling ocean. . . . Peal after peal rattled over our heads, with a sound which seemed actually to stop the breath in the body, and the "speedy gleams" kept the whole ocean in a glare of light. . . . During all which time there was not a breath stirring, and we lay motionless, like a mark to be shot at . . . The rain fell at intervals in heavy showers, and we stood drenched through and blinded by the flashes, which broke the Egyptian darkness with a brightness which seemed almost malignant; while the thunder rolled in peals, the concussion of which appeared to shake the very ocean. (329)

Less than a month remained of the arduous voyage home, but curious weather from the West Indies to Bermuda assailed them; and Captain Thompson, who had married shortly before leaving Boston and so "it may be supposed . . . was not slow in carrying sail" (332), gave the experienced old salts aboard ample evidence to judge him to be abusive of his ship. To complete Dana's maritime education, scurvy broke out next; and among others, Ben, the English lad who nearly replaced Dana on the *Pilgrim,* came down with it in a particularly virulent form. He was cured by being fed a juicy paste of raw potatoes and raw onions fortunately obtained south of Bermuda from a passing brig. Next the men braced for an expected storm off Cape Hatteras, but it failed to materialize. By September 15 they were entering the Gulf Stream, which induced the previously noted swaying of the vessel and the accompanying nausea of most of the hands, even the oldest. The last challenge Dana met at sea was the trial of going aloft for two hours to work on the reeling royal-masthead; clearly, he was now the ablest seaman of them all.

On September 16 the ship was in the latitude of Washington, D.C., though ten degrees east and hence far out to sea; but a steady southwester was carrying her ever nearer home. On September 17 the light wind breezed up toward nightfall, and Captain Thompson soon had a chance to show some good seamanship: he picked his way through thick fog by soundings alone—southeast of Block Island on September 18, near George's Banks the next morning (after grazing a Bristol whaler), by that night north toward the Chatham lights, and then at daybreak on September 20 "there lay the low sand-hills of Cape Cod, over our larboard quarter, and before us, the wide waters of Massachusetts Bay, with here and there a sail gliding over its smooth surface" (340-41). That evening the already mentioned listlessness settled upon Dana, and he stood on the deck with memories of his magical two-year adventure vying with ambitious thoughts about his immediate future.

CHAPTER 3

Variable Weather, 1836-1855

BACK IN BOSTON, Dana had three problems—what to do about his spiritual condition, how to proceed with his formal education, and what to decide on for his future profession. His solutions and their consequences carried him so far away from the sailor he had been, even though he wrote about his nautical adventures, that before long he looked back on California as the scene of an extended boyish prank.

I *To the Right*

The Danas had long been conservative Congregationalists and had stood against the liberals during the Unitarian Schism of 1829.[1] Later Dana somewhat regretted this fact, as he shows in a letter to his eleven-year-old son:

> I wish I had had, when a boy of your age, the teachings and exercises of the Episcopal Church. But our family were then all Congregationalists and held certain views of God and religion known as Calvinism, which were very repulsive and hard. And we young people took no interest in the Church. There were no interesting services,—no Easter, no Lent, no Good Friday, no liturgy. You have great privileges in all these respects, and religion, though made serious, as it ought to be, is not austere and repulsive.[2]

What Dana really wanted was a combination of conservative Christian doctrine and a bit of medieval pageantry.

Shortly after returning to Boston from the antipodes, Dana was intensely moved when he heard that Sarah Woods, his Andover tutor's sister and a former girlfriend of his, had prayed deliriously just before her death for his immortal soul. Soon thereafter, having gone through a period of spiritual prostration the way the youthful Jonathan Edwards did, Dana "sought pardon through Christ as the appointed way, & by uniting myself with the visible Church, & partaking of his ordinances, & seeking knowledge of eternal things, began, I trust, that religious life which I have since followed. God knows & my own soul knows how lamely, miserably & sinfully, but yet I trust with a hope of heaven & of seeing & enjoying God hereafter."[3] This step led to his being confirmed a year and a half later in the Episcopal Cathedral Church of St. Paul, Boston.[4]

Dana re-entered Harvard College three months after returning from sea. He studied intensively for a preparatory examination, joined the class of 1837, and was promised his degree the following spring by cooperative President Josiah Quincy. The young man worked hard, was academically and socially most successful, and would have been valedictorian of the class except that his truncated record was quite irregular. After all, he had attended school only about seven months in the academic year 1831-32 and had then been suspended until the following fall, at which time he had been forced from all study by weak eyes. So he should have counted himself fortunate to obtain a Harvard degree for about twelve months of residence, and for some private reading under Leonard Woods, Jr., of Andover.

But Dana deserved his honors, which included election to Phi Beta Kappa and admission to both of Harvard's social clubs, the Porcellian and the Hasty Pudding. Moreover, he won prizes for declaiming effectively against the Reform Bill and for grinding out an essay on Edward Bulwer-Lytton's novels. His graduation dissertation, commendably delivered, took the Wordsworthian text that "Heaven lies about us in our infancy." Dana gave it a significant twist by arguing with both hesitant realism and also pseudo-mysticism that the young child hates to have reality—which, of course, must be faced—break in on him, and that the oldster recollects the visionary pleasures of childhood with serenity. And he pointed toward *Two Years Before the Mast* in this hardheaded line: "the storm—to others so full of terror and sublimity—to the sailor means nothing but a wet jacket & a sleepless night."[5] Dana was always a combination of romantic and realist.

Never thinking seriously of being an idle man of letters like his father, Dana chose to emulate more vigorous forebears and become a lawyer. His choice of profession, like his choices of school and church, indicates the conservative drift of his mind, which increased over the years. He feared that the law would be inflexible and dull, but he was most fortunate in being able to study under a small faculty which included Judge Joseph Story and Professor Simon Greenleaf of the Dane Law School at Harvard. These men regarded the law as Christian, as ethically challenging, as profoundly philosophical, and as intellectually competitive.

From the start, Dana was encouraged to feel superior to the hurly-burly of mere courtroom fighting: "Free from all the details, chicanery & responsibilities of practice [he later wrote], we were placed in a library, under learned, honourable & gentlemanly instructors, & invited to pursue the study of jurisprudence, as a system of philosophy."[6] After a year of such theory, Dana began pleading cases in moot court and annotating the arguments of his fellow students and the decisions of his professors. At the same time, Dana kept up a rigorous program of outside reading— the Bible, Greek, Latin, French, German, logic, mathematics, and history.[7] In addition, through the year of 1838 he evidently wrote his first draft of most of *Two Years Before the Mast.*[8] Then in January, 1839, while still attending law school, he began teaching elocution at Harvard.

In February, 1840, Dana resigned his teaching post and left the law school to enter the office of a Boston lawyer. After gaining much valuable practical experience in seven months there, Dana was admitted to the bar and at once opened his first office, at 20 Court Street. By mid-September his *Two Years Before the Mast* was published, "not because I supposed the book could be of much benefit to me in a literary or pecuniary point of view [Dana later noted], but because I thought it would be of some use to me in Boston in securing to me a share of maritime business, in insurance & other maritime cases, & because I believed it would also do something to enlighten the public as to the real situation of common seamen in the merchant service."[9]

Whether the book was of much direct aid to oppressed seamen or not is a moot question, but it assuredly brought its author much legal work. According to Charles Francis Adams, Jr., who later read law under Dana and was his first biographer, "In those days, and indeed long afterwards, his office was apt to be crowded with unkept, roughly dressed seamen, and it smelled on such occasions much like a forecastle; but he was young and in earnest, and to a young lawyer anything is preferable to that unbroken waiting which is apt to mark the beginning of professional life."[10] In fact, the young lawyer was soon doing so well that he moved into an office in the old State House building, hired a student-assistant, and began to think of marriage.

Back in the summer of 1838 an old family friend who had been visiting briefly in Cambridge had brought with him two nieces. One of them was Miss Sarah Watson, nicknamed "Sally," the daughter of an impoverished Hartford merchant. Struck at once by her handsome figure, gracefulness, and lady-like gentility, Dana contrived after she returned home to keep up a correspondence with her until the following summer, at which time he used the excuse of attending his brother Ned's graduation from the University of Vermont at Burlington to see Miss Watson again and even to accompany her by steamer to New York and then Albany, where she and her party met her brother. Friendship soon developed into love, and love with Sarah Watson evidently included spiritual mortification. Early in his married life, Dana recalled that "It was a trial I needed, & I stood the test, & years of happiness than which man cannot have greater from a fellow mortal have been my exceeding reward."[11]

Dana and Sarah Watson were married on August 25, 1841, in Hartford. After a brief honeymoon in Rockport, Massachusetts, they made their first home in the United States Hotel in Boston.

II Two Years Before the Mast—*Composition and Reception*

By the time of his marriage, Dana was a busy maritime lawyer and also a lecturer much in demand from Maine to Maryland because of the popularity of *Two Years Before the Mast*. In his *Autobiographical Sketch* he says that he wrote it during his last two years in law school, 1838 and 1839. But Professor Robert F. Lucid presents evidence to suggest that most of the manuscript was finished by Christmas, 1838. On the basis of a detailed examination of the manuscript, now deposited with the Massachusetts Historical Society, Lucid concludes that the composition probably proceeded in three stages: a rapidly written draft with deletions; then, after a rereading, more deletions and also interleavings; and, finally, a minor touching up. Dana evidently relied only on his memory, probably a few of his letters saved at home, and his ten-leaf sea journal, in the margins of which he penciled notes reminding himself of topics to be written up when he felt that they should be worked in.[12]

To avoid giving offense to certain readers and perhaps by this time to Miss Watson and even himself, Dana in reworking the manuscript cut out some of the oaths and his comments on venereal disease, drunkenness, and smuggling in California; added his regrets concerning misspent liberty Sundays; reduced the number of similes comparing ships to horses; and revised his transcription of Hawaiian words.[13] Unfortunately, at this time he was drifting back to conservative literary Romanticism instead of steering toward incipient Realism, as every modern reader of *Two Years Before the Mast* surely wishes he had done. Most of Dana's deletions and marginal additions appear, therefore, in the direction of propriety rather than raw honesty. His stated purpose may have been to present "the light and the dark [of a sailor's life] together,"[14] but his increasing respect for religious, family, social, and academic traditions kept *Two Years Before the Mast* from being a startling contribution to Realism. Its author aimed simply to present a true picture of life at sea. He wanted to entertain his readers and perhaps also move them. He evidently cared nothing about popular fame as a mere literary artist, since he wanted at most his initials—not his full name—to appear on the title page.[15] But he assuredly hoped that his book would indirectly result in the material and spiritual betterment of sailors everywhere.

Even while he drifted toward Romanticism, however, Dana also remembered the admonitions of his professor of rhetoric and oratory, Edward Tyrrel Channing, who had taught him—and Thoreau as well—to write clearly and naturally. Therefore some of the emendations in the draft of *Two Years Before the Mast* resulted in a greater degree of simplicity. Since his intention was to reproduce the actual feel of his experiences, he also deleted certain details which he would not have thought of while a certain event was happening or which he could not have known until long after it.

When the book was almost ready for publication, Leonard Woods, Jr., took the manuscript to New York in May, 1839, to try to interest the Harper brothers in it. Dana's father asked William

Cullen Byrant to glance at it and was stupid enough to add that the influential poet should feel free to place it without any thought of possible profit. The Harper brothers tentatively offered Dana a 10 per cent royalty after the first one thousand copies had been sold. Richard Henry Dana, Sr., empowered by his son to act in any way he wished concerning the whole matter, rejected this proposal.[16] When Dana finished the introduction and concluding chapter, in February, 1840, and sent back the revised manuscript, the Harper brothers asked one of their readers, Alonzo Potter—then a philosophy and political economics professor at Union College, in Schenectady, New York, and later bishop of Pennsylvania—to pass judgment on it. Potter later told Dana that he had advised acceptance at any price. The Harper company made one more offer and stuck to it: two hundred and fifty dollars plus twenty-four copies for all rights. Dana's father and Bryant tried in vain to hold out for five hundred dollars, then three hundred; but then, instead of sensibly seeking a more generous publisher, they finally accepted the Harper brothers' terms.[17]

The book was an instantaneous success. Dana estimated that it yielded its publishers a profit of ten thousand dollars in the first two years and perhaps as much as fifty thousand dollars during the whole period of the original copyright—until 1869.[18] *Two Years Before the Mast* netted Dana more in its first British edition than his two-hundred-and-fifty-dollar American payment. Charles Sumner, the future Free Soil Senator, and Fanny Appleton, who was later Henry Wadsworth Longfellow's second wife, sent copies of it to friends in England, where it soon happened to catch the sharp eye of Edward Moxon, the British publisher. He brought out *Two Years Before the Mast* in London, sold twelve thousand copies the first year, and generously sent Dana five hundred dollars, although, in the absence of any international copyright laws, he need not have paid him anything.[19]

In 1841 Dana wrote and published *The Seaman's Friend*—reprinted in England as *The Seaman's Manual*—a popular book on seamanship, customs at sea, and the rights and duties of masters and sailors afloat and ashore. When the nation was rocked by the *Somers* mutiny in 1843, Dana was asked to look into the entire *cause célèbre* and to prepare for publication a long letter containing his impressions. He did so, and the report is full of implications that this lawyer and veteran of the merchant service was also an expert on naval matters. The fact that Dana's opinion was sought proves that his *Two Years Before the Mast* was not only phenomenally popular but also highly influential.

It was reviewed at once as a brilliant piece of truthful—but not artistic—reporting. Emerson and Bryant, among others, regarded it as powerful propaganda and used it as a springboard to launch into expressions of hope for maritime reform. Over the years the unfounded opinion developed that, as Van Wyck Brooks cavalierly summarizes it, *Two Years Before the Mast* "had done as much for the sailors as Dickens had done for the debtors and orphans of England and *Uncle Tom's Cabin* for the slaves."[20] Professor Lucid forcefully presents the other side: *Two Years Before the Mast* is a picture of the light and dark of a sailor's life but not in any sense a tract written with any reform in mind.[21] Lucid's reasoned conclusion is that "There is simply no evidence that *Two Years* caused strong public indignation of any lasting sort. . . . The book provided some material for the already strong [reform] societies, and was, at best, grist for the current reform mill."[22] Following Lucid, Professor Samuel Shapiro asserts that "Evidence available from the book itself, and from Dana's later career, . . . proves that the book was not intended to be a plea for reform. The story of the flogging takes up only six pages out of some four hundred and fifty; from the rest of the book one gets the impression that the crews with whom Dana sailed, while they worked hard and had scant leisure, were on the whole fairly well treated."[23]

The truth would appear to lie somewhere between Brooks on the one side, and Lucid and Shapiro on the other. The position is certainly no longer tenable that *Two Years Before the Mast* is the *Uncle Tom's Cabin* of the high seas. However, the indirect influence of Dana's book on would-be reformers was of the sort that must forever be incalculable while nonetheless definite. As for what Dana, deep down, really intended his book to be, it would take a bold critic or an irresponsible speculator to say with certainty and in detail. But it is true that, while Dana was forced to stand helplessly by and watch two of his mates brutally flogged by a dancing sadist, he vowed to do something to redress the grievances of sailors and to relieve their sufferings. One of his intentions when he published his book must surely have been to do just that. Further, it is naïve to say that Dana and his mates were "fairly well treated." If *Two Years Before the Mast* is accurate, they must have been treated more like animals than men. Professor Elmo Paul Hohman, an expert on maritime matters, summarizes life in the American merchant service in the middle of the nineteenth century: "Hours were long and often irregular . . . Wages were low . . . Discipline was harsh, brutal, and subjective, with many abuses. Food and living conditions were inadequate at the best and inhuman and unbelievable at the worst. Working conditions represented a composite of danger, hardship, privation, adventure, monotony, complete subjection to authority, pitiless driving, and (sometimes) a certain fascination and joy in life at sea."[24] Dana might have summarized his maritime experience in precisely the same words.

In England the worth of *Two Years Before the Mast* was demonstrated by uniformly favorable reviews, which praised it for its straightforward, simple, documentary style and for the good its contents would do. More important to Dana, it opened the doors to high society for him when he went to England in 1856 and again later. He was not especially impressed when a common fellow like Charles Dickens wanted to meet him in Boston or when a chap of Anthony Trollope's station in life published praise of his book in the *North American Review*. Much later, when Dana went to England, he was of course delighted that his book had preceded him and thus helped to make him feel welcome.

III *Reaching for Greatness*

The many exciting activities of Dana from 1842 until his first trip to England—in fact, until the eve of the Civil War—are easy to trace, thanks to his voluminous *Journal,* which totals more than half a million words and which has just been published for the first time in full. Dana started it on December 17, 1841, and faithfully kept it until he returned from his trip around the world in the fall of 1860. With the exception of his brief trip to Cuba early in 1859, Dana recorded the details of his major activities in his *Journal;* in addition, it often contains descriptions of lesser events—public, professional, and personal—and is hence a mine of information about the man. Two conclusions can be drawn from studying it: Dana solidly supported the law and tried always to strengthen it and to apply it humanely but strictly; and he also fought one losing battle after another, stiffly and with bad timing, but hard and honorably as well. His *Journal* shows us his defeats and pleasures; and we gain from it added respect for Dana as a man of high standards and as an observant, forceful writer.

Five events of considerable importance to Dana at this time were the *Somers* mutiny of 1842 and the subsequent court-martial of the commander of the *Somers;* the rousing National Free Soil Convention held in Buffalo in 1848; the so-called "Rescue Trials" of several persons accused of helping to free Shadrach, the fugitive slave apprehended in Boston in 1851; the 1853 Massachusetts Constitutional Convention held at Boston; and the infamous rendition back into slavery of Anthony Burns of Boston in 1854. Dana recorded all of these events, as well as his often considerable part in them, in his *Journal.*

The *Somers* mutiny was a dreadful affair, which stirred up expressions of fiery resentment of both sides. The *Somers*, a 266-ton naval brig under the command of Alexander Slidell Mackenzie, who had a handful of officers and about a hundred men, was returning from Africa in November, 1842, when her crew was shaken by strong rumors of a mutiny supposedly planned by an irresponsible, hotheaded midshipman named Philip Spencer. When Commander Mackenzie first heard of the plot, he discounted it until evidence was presented which satisfied him. Then he and his seven officers met and quickly prepared and signed a document ordering the immediate execution of Spencer and two of his cohorts. On December 1, the three were hanged. Two circumstances were adverse to Mackenzie's position: in the first place, at the time of the hanging the *Somers* was only 525 miles from the Virgin Islands; and in the second place, young Spencer was the son of Secretary of War John C. Spencer, of President John Tyler's Cabinet. So, when the captain sailed into New York a week or so later, a court of inquiry convened, and he was court-martialed but exonerated.

Many writers voiced the sentiments of innumerable outraged Americans, who unprofessionally argued that the captain could surely have clapped irons upon the ringleaders of the mutiny, if indeed there were any, and brought them to land and a full investigation. But Dana, both in his *Journal* and in a long open letter published in several newspapers beginning on January 11, 1843, defended Mackenzie. Dana pointed out that Mackenzie was a distinguished officer and scholar, that the *Somers* was so tiny that half a dozen determined mutineers could have killed and tossed every officer overboard in three minutes, that the officers' quarters were too cramped to be defended, that the crew was both large and inexperienced, that the rebels had been defiant of authority and surreptitiously armed, that there was strong evidence of a plot, and that the officers were pledged to protect the threatened brig and to see to it that she did not become a pirate ship. Moreover, some of the most favorable evidence on Mackenzie's side pointed to the conclusion that Spencer seems to have been a completely unbalanced young scamp who long had used his father's name to scare off opposition and who did want to become a pirate.[25]

In his writings on the *Somers* affair, Dana emerges as a tough-minded upholder of the letter of the law. If a captain at sea suspects mutiny, he has the right and obligation to take all reasonable steps necessary to protect his vessel and those men under him who are unquestionably loyal.[26]

During the next few years Dana prospered, moved into a larger law office at 30 Court Street, took a skillful partner, Francis Edward Parker (who remained with him until 1861), and began to quarrel intermittently with his wife Sarah.[27] Then in 1848, seeing the possibility of distinguishing himself in the newly emerging Free Soil party, Dana went to its national convention in August at Buffalo. Professor Shapiro overstates the case by suggesting that the normally non-radical Dana stopped being aloof from various reform movements and, rather like a would-be malcontent seeking a cause, fastened upon the Free Soil movement.[28] The truth is that Dana always favored freedom under the law and also could hardly have successfully entered national politics much earlier than at the age of thirty-three. The Free Soil movement in 1848 was appealing to him; and, having a reliable associate in Frank Parker, he was able to attend the Buffalo convention without much loss of income.

Dana was a Daniel Webster Whig until just before he went to Buffalo. Then, at considerable cost to himself socially and professionally, he abandoned the bandwagon of General Zachary Taylor, the Whig candidate; Dana returned home from the con-

Variable Weather, 1836-1855

vention, which had nominated former President Martin Van Buren and Charles Francis Adams on the Free Soil ticket, to find himself so ostracized that he took to the lecture circuit in and around Boston to explain his position with his famous speech, "Buffalo Free Soil Convention, 1848." But feeling in Boston ran so high that, in spite of his sensible speech, Dana was snubbed on the street and lost several clients because most Bostonians at that time did not wish to disturb the uneasy alliance of Southern cotton and Northern mills.

A few years later, after his brilliant work at the Massachusetts Constitutional Convention, Dana was asked to explain his surprising affiliation with the Free Soilers; and his letter of reply made four succinct points. First, he was a Free Soiler by inheritance, since he was the son and grandson of Federalists who had always opposed the extension of slavery into the Northwest Territory. Second, he was a Free Soiler by education, having been brought up among the faction of Whigs steadily supporting the Free Soil movement. Third, he backed the movement though his inherent conservatism, which, unlike Hunkerism and Radicalism both, was in his view based on high-minded, antimaterialistic moral principles. And fourth, he was a Free Soiler because he hated to see his fine New England stock placed at the service of the Southern slave-holding oligarchy, even if his position meant debits instead of credits on the ledgers of Boston.[29] Then came Dana's conclusion:

> Having said so much, I will add that I take you literally. You mean "Free Soiler" and nothing else. A technical Abolitionist I am not. I am a constitutionalist, and in favor of adhering honestly to all the compromises of that instrument. If I were in Congress, and the South should come into court with clean hands, keeping faithfully her side of the compact, and demand of us a fugitive slave law, I should feel bound to give her one (either by national or state legislation), and a *bona fide* one, but one consistent with law, decency, safety to the free, and the self-respect of the North.[30]

For the next several years Dana and his partner had plenty of law work, in spite of an attempted boycott of the firm by Bostonians opposed to his Free Soil inclinations. He became notoriously successful in maritime work, sometimes aiding seamen seeking back pay or damages, but more often defending companies in salvage cases, insurance matters, and the like. Then, just as he was beginning to be looked upon as reliable again, the 1851 "Rescue Trials" exploded.

The Compromise of 1850, among its other accomplishments, obliged Northern law-enforcement officers to be more efficient in returning fugitive slaves. As the center of the Abolition movement, Boston inevitably was the scene in which the Compromise was destined to be tested. The first such affair came when Frederick Wilkins, a Bible-spouting Negro nicknamed "Shadrach," escaped from his Virginia master, got a job as a waiter in Boston, and was arrested as a fugitive slave on February 15, 1851. Dana instantly repaired to the courthouse across the street from his office; advised with Robert Morris, Shadrach's Negro lawyer; prepared a petition for a writ of habeas corpus; and grew furious when Judge Lemuel Shaw contemptuously and illogically refused the petition. Then circumstances made it unnecessary for Dana to continue a legal paper battle: the same afternoon Shadrach was bodily carried into freedom by a pair of stalwart rescuers. He ultimately got to Canada safely. In his *Journal* Dana could not help applauding:

> . . . we heard a shout from the court-house, continued into a yell of triumph, and in an instant after down the steps came two huge negroes bearing the prisoner between them with his clothes half torn off, & so stupefied by the sudden rescue and the violence of his dragging off that he sat almost dumb, and I thought had fainted; but the men seized him, and being powerful fellows hurried him through the square into Court Street, where he found the use of his feet, and they went off toward Cambridge, like a black squall, the crowd driving along with them and cheering as they went. It was all done in an instant, too quick to be believed, and so successful was it that not only was no negro arrested, but no attempt was made at pursuit. . . .
>
> How can any right-minded man do else than rejoice at the rescue of a man from the hopeless, endless slavery to which a recovered fugitive is always doomed. If the law were constitutional, which I firmly believe it is not, it would be the duty of a citizen not to resist it by force, unless he was prepared for revolution and civil war; but we rejoice in the escape of a victim of an unjust law, as we would in the escape of an ill-treated captive deer or bird.[31]

Dana soon had his chance to fight, legally and in court, against the vicious excesses of the law he considered unconstitutional. The discomfited defenders of the Fugitive Slave Law, led by Daniel Webster himself, were so determined to sacrifice a scapegoat that they actually arrested Charles G. Davis and Robert Morris, both of whom were Shadrach's lawyers, and charged them with conspiring in their client's whirlwind escape. Dana volunteered to defend them at half his usual fee, and he also earned the usual amount of abuse from the Cotton Whigs all about. His courtroom performance included one of his most stirring speeches, and he made everyone, from timid judge down to pusillanimous deputies, listen to his blistering blast at the Fugitive Slave Law. As Dana modestly wrote his brother afterward, "I made a speech . . . of five hours. It was the best thing I ever did, under the most favorable circumstances, & with the most successful results."[32]

A month later Dana became informally involved in the case of Thomas Sims, another fugitive slave, apprehended like Shadrach but unlike him returned to bondage. Sims resisted arrest by stabbing a policeman. Judge Shaw, giving a little speech against slavery, nonetheless again refused to issue a writ which would have aided Sims. Webster spoke moodily against Sims and in favor of the Fugitive Slave Law. Thomas Higginson and Theodore Parker unsuccessfully planned to rescue Sims from his courthouse room by wile or force. The pressure of other office work made it impossible for Dana to continue advising Sims, who was eventually escorted by a Boston deputy all the way to Savannah, where he was beaten and then sold.

Dana next deserted his busy office from May 4 to August 1, 1853, to participate in the Massachusetts Constitutional Convention, held in Boston. Easily elected from Manchester, the little town in which the Danas had a summer house, he quickly established himself as a forceful independent: nominally he represented the Free Soilers but often seemed on the side of the conservative Whigs. Professor Shapiro, who takes many occasions to criticize the actions of Dana here and elsewhere, does call him "The only leading man in the convention who rose above partisanship."[33]

Once again, his high principles cost him. While the Boston Whigs began to congratulate Dana on his return to conservative sanity, the progressives who had sent him to the convention felt that he was letting them down. He favored retaining the system of appointing judges for indefinite terms—so long as they were not derelict in their duties—and spoke eloquently against electing them or appointing them for short terms. His speech on the subject drew unprecedented praise from Rufus Choate. Dana also objected to dividing Massachusetts into representative districts strictly on the basis of population, since doing so would hurt the small towns. He seemingly feared the increasing strength of big cities, whose populations were being swelled by hordes of immigrants. His stand led to a violent argument with George S. Hillard, who reminded Dana in an offensive public speech that he should not strike the hand—namely, Boston—that fed him. Dana literally leaped at the challenge. "The hand that feeds us! The hand that feeds us! *Sir, no hand feeds me that has any right to control my opinions!*"[34]

Late in June, Dana was highly honored at the convention. As he noted in his *Journal,* "The grand committee of thirteen is appointed to reduce the Constitution to the form of articles. I am upon it, and it consists, of course, of the leading men of all parties. This committee has referred the resolves to a sub-committee of three, Governor [George S.] Boutwell, Judge [Joel] Parker and myself, so that we shall be the actual writers of the new parts of the Constitution."[35] Dana attended all regular convention meetings and then slaved away with Boutwell until midnight and sometimes much later. The response to the astutely revised Constitution was that it was narrowly rejected at the polls by about 5,000 votes out of 130,000.[36] Dana was miserably depressed by the vote.

Soon events conspired to make him a hero in the eyes of his Boston compatriots—and almost a martyr. The celebrated Anthony Burns case of May and June, 1854, was the occasion. Burns, another fugitive slave, had been identified by his master, Colonel Charles Suttle, and arrested on May 24 by a gang of deputies. The next morning Dana learned that Burns was penned up in the courthouse and instantly volunteered to defend the apathetic fellow, who, however, was too terrified by the sight of Suttle to agree. Dana went ahead anyway and effected a two-day delay in the court hearing, during which time Boston became violently aroused in the fugitive's favor. Hotheads who had been legally worsted in the Sims affair were predictably uglier now, and many former neutrals had been swung out of their pro-Southern complacency and into the other camp by the Nebraska Act. While Wendell Phillips and Theodore Parker orated, Higginson foolishly led a charge up the courthouse steps, during which a man fired at a marshal but missed, a volunteer guard was fatally stabbed in the groin, and Higginson himself was slashed across the face. The police had to be aided by redoubtable marines mustered from nearby, and President Franklin Pierce himself ordered the law to be mercilessly enforced.

Hating such unconstitutional tactics as his friends were executing, Dana had himself appointed Burns's lawyer and instantly set his own finer strategy into motion. Meanwhile, Southern students from Harvard formed a bodyguard for Suttle. Several Northerners began raising money to buy Burns back into liberty. Suttle happily accepted twelve hundred dollars and was about to hand over the release papers when United States District Attorney Benjamin Franklin Hallett intervened. After all, one policeman had been killed and a good deal of federal money already spent: Hallett therefore felt obliged to nullify the sale so that a trial could add to the solemnity of the affair.

Fully as much as Burns, Dana was the hero of the wretched case. He brilliantly pounced upon every last stupidity of Suttle's cocksure lawyer, used the entire affair as an opportunity to harangue against the Fugitive Slave Law, and eloquently insulted the massed opposition. Shapiro praises Dana's action and then expertly summarizes his position:

> Although he [Dana] believed the Fugitive Slave Law unconstitutional, principally because it failed to provide for a jury trial, he was willing to accept the contrary judgment of state and federal courts. But he insisted all the more tenaciously on giving the escaped Negro every advantage possible under the law. If the claimant could not prove the identity of the fugitive beyond a reasonable doubt, the Commissioner ought to declare the accused a free man. If legally unimpeachable evidence against an escaped slave could be produced, however, Dana was willing to acquiesce in his return to slavery. Although he sympathized with the victim, Dana was unwilling to see him rescued by violence, or even saved by an unconstitutional Personal Liberty law. . . .
>
> In the America of the 1850's such a calm, conservative

attitude was increasingly rare. . . . Many men were willing to cast aside traditional legal safeguards in order to propitiate the South, and still more could be found to rescue fugitive slaves by violence. Men of Dana's calm and sober disposition were exceedingly scarce, at a time when the country had most need of them.[37]

Dana's closing speech in the Burns case was one of his most rhetorical, impassioned, and acute. But poor Burns was returned to Virginia from a groaning, grieving Boston which had to be held in check by soldiers with rifles, bayonets, and swords. Several men in the irate crowd were kicked and sabred by the militia ordered out to protect Southern property rights in Burns, who solemnly marched down to the wharf where a revenue cutter was waiting for him. Boston draped itself in black, as though for the funeral of human rights.

One of the casualties was Dana himself. On June 2, the day of the adverse decision in court, he was not even permitted to say farewell to his client Burns without having the marshal's men standing nearby to eavesdrop. When his request to walk with Burns to the ship was denied, the two men quietly shook hands and separated. After Burns was gone, Dana returned to his office to do some paperwork until evening. Then he had tea with a friend at a hotel. As he was walking about 9:30, with his friend along Court Street toward Bowdoin Square, intending to go out to Cambridge on foot, he was suddenly slugged from behind. As Dana describes it,

. . . I remember observing a commotion on my left as of people pushing, and instantly I received a terrible blow over my right eye. I was stunned by it for a moment. Whether I was knocked down or not I do not know. I first remember standing in the street, stupefied and bleeding, and thinking that I had been hit by some accident. I thought that an iron bar which is used to confine window shutters had been suddenly thrown out and had hit me, or that I had received a chance blow from some one in a quarrel at my side. I saw no man. The blow was from behind or at my side, and I do not distinctly remember seeing anything go across my sight, though I have some indistinct recollection of something like an arm or a stick passing across my sight. People came about me, and I recollect insisting upon it that I was not hit intentionally, until several told me they saw the man and the blow, and then I said to [Anson] Burlingame [Dana's companion], "Well, we've kept the field." I walked to Dr. Slater's with Burlingame, where he left me, to go to the police office to lodge a complaint, and to the newspapers. Dr. Slater applied arnica externally for nearly an hour, reducing the swelling considerably. The weight of the blow fortunately fell on the strong bone over the eye and on the cheek bone. If it had hit the eye, it would have destroyed it. If it had hit the temple, I have little doubt it would have broken it in.[38]

Dana, who had come close to being killed, was fortunately almost well again within a week. By that time his assailant, an ex-boxer named Henry Huxford, was behind bars. Louis Varrell, a gangster who had scraped together the scum of Boston to assemble the marshal's guard around Burns, had taken umbrage when Dana remarked in his closing speech that, since Varrell's men were busy in court, the good citizens of Boston were leaving their doors unlocked at night and the brothels were untenanted by men. Varrell bided his time; and, when his gang was disbanded, he treated a dozen of them in a saloon near the courthouse and then, pointing out his enemy Dana to them, said colorfully, "I'll give any man ten dollars who will give him his corn"[39]—and Huxford had accepted the offer.

At his trial, Huxford foolishly tried to deny knowing who Dana was, until Dana's lawyer asked him if he were not one of the marshal's guards, who had necessarily heard all of Dana's courtroom speeches. When Varrell obligingly posted bail in the amount of fifteen hundred dollars for his thug, Huxford returned the favor by disappearing. This action was, of course, a violation of such honor as exists among thieves; so Varrell produced two eyewitnesses to the attack on Dana. Their testimony was taken, and Varrell next put a shrewd private detective on the trial of Huxford, who was soon returned from New Orleans to Boston, to trial, and to a two-year jail sentence.

Of the two witnesses who had sealed Huxford's doom, Dana recorded in his *Journal* that "It was refreshing to the sight to behold two such clean, straight, comely, nicely dressed youths. . . . The absence of anything dashing or overdressed about them was noticeable. Their manners were models of quietude and self-possession. Each told his story simply and clearly . . ."[40] Dana began to feel a touch of sympathy for Huxford, "the poor, blundering brute as against his clever and wickeder master, Varrell."[41] Of the latter he wrote that "Varrell moved among his crowd with a higher crown and a longer sceptre than ever."[42]

Two years later Dana learned that Huxford was out of prison and desired to drop into his office for a friendly chat. Dana agreed, and he probably felt somewhat superior and forgiving, and in addition perhaps a trifle brave. As Dana records the whole fascinating episode with much narrative zest in his *Journal,* the ex-convict amicably told Dana the whole story: he confessed that he had indeed delivered the near-fatal blow but then revealed that Varrell's two clean-cut witnesses were hired perjurers. This fact was corroborated when one of the two, blinded in one eye by a vindictive friend of Huxford's, later went to Dana and told his part in the affair. He then asked Dana for legal assistance in recovering an inheritance in Vermont, and Dana was generous—or naïve—enough to give the man money to go north in search of his legacy.[43]

CHAPTER 4

Three Voyages, 1856-1860

D ANA SPENT THE next five or six years in gargantuan labor
and princely leisure. During the summer of 1855 he and a
few others decided to establish the splendid Saturday Club. Dana
was virtually a charter member of this illustrious group, which
in the beginning included Louis Agassiz, Ralph Waldo Emerson,
James Russell Lowell, John Lothrop Motley, Edwin Percy Whip-
ple, and several others, and later such additional luminaries as
Nathaniel Hawthorne, Oliver Wendell Holmes, William Dean
Howells, Henry James, Sr., Henry Wadsworth Longfellow, Francis Parkman, William Hickling Prescott, Charles Sumner, and
John Greenleaf Whittier. In his *Journal,* Dana writes only briefly
and tardily about the club.

> I believe I have no where mentioned the Club. It has become
> an important and much valued thing to us. . . . We have no
> written rules, and keep no records. Our only object is to dine
> together once a month. Our day is the last Saturday in every
> month, and we dine at Parker's. A unanimous vote is required
> to elect a member. The expense of the dinner is assessed
> upon those present, and charged at the office, so we have
> no money affairs to attend to. Guests are permitted, but each
> man pays for the guest he invites. . . . The Club had an
> accidental origin, in a habit of Emerson, Dwight, Whipple
> and one or two more dining at Woodman's room at Parker's
> occasionally; for Woodman is a bachelor, a literary quidnunc
> and gossip, or as Gould says, "a genius broker." Ward is a
> friend of Emerson's, and came. From this the club grew,
> Ward, Dwight, Woodman, Whipple and Emerson being the
> originals. Agassiz, Peirce and I were early invited to meet
> with them. This made it more of a regular thing, and we
> established our verbal rule as to membership, guests and
> expenses. Lowell came in soon after, and then Motley and
> Longfellow. The first formal vote we had for members was

at this stage, for up to this time unanimous consent was obtained by conversation. The vote brought in Holmes and Felton, which made the number fourteen, as many as we think it best to have.[1] (August 6, 1857)*

This club, as well as other social activities, helped alleviate Dana's hideous office pressure. In addition, on three separate occasions he was obliged to get away from all work for extended periods of time.

I *To England and France and Back*

Dana went to England and, briefly, to France, in July and August, 1856. The time for his visit was especially propitious. He was at the top of his powers intellectually. His mind had been largely formed by English theologians, philosophers, legal writers, and men of letters; yet he had never seen England. His fame as the author of *Two Years Before the Mast,* as a Free Soiler, and as the defender of Anthony Burns preceded him. His friendship with Charles Sumner was also well known; and Sumner, perhaps more highly regarded by important Britishers than any other American alive, was happy to furnish Dana, as well as other friends, with reams of introductory letters. Finally, Victorian England in 1856 was officially as rigidly righteous as Dana would have wished it always to remain.[2]

Dana's *Journal* from July 2 until September 3, 1856, is a low-keyed paean of unmitigated delight. The oppressedly busy man got away from wife (then some six weeks pregnant), family, and office. He was at sea again for the first extended period of time in twenty years, bound for the Europe of his dreams (July 2). For the first time his keen eyes soon rested on Ireland, Scotland, and gently tinted European skies. As he rode the train to London, he grew ecstatic over the ever-changing but unendingly thrilling English countryside.

This city, which he called the greatest in Christendom (July 18), was a cornucopia of pleasures to Dana; he untiringly inspected twenty or more of its main landmarks, including the Tower, during his first full day there. During the first few days he set himself a dizzy pace, which tourists a century and more

---

* Dates in parentheses in this section refer to entries in Dana's *Journal.*

later would find it hard to emulate even with the ostensible advantages of automobile, omnibus, and underground.

In the company of Lord Elgin, Dana visited the British Museum, which for size and munificence he found impossible to describe (July 26). He was a bit disappointed with St. Paul's, but the Crystal Palace was a uniquely memorable thrill (July 31). After visiting the famous wine vaults of the London Docks, he was exact enough to record that the port wine comprised eleven acres (July 28). He grew unabashedly emotional in the Poets' Corner of Westminster Abbey, to which he returned again and again on crowded Sundays for church service and at other times when it was as lonely and melancholy as Washington Irving had earlier found it often to be. On one occasion Dana notes, however, that it was glorious and subduing (July 27).

He haunted also the Houses of Parliament, visited the National Gallery, Regent's Park and other spots of green in the heart of London, and went out to Hampton Court. And he quickly ranged farther afield: to Windsor, Eton, Stoke Poges (which he called the heart of England—July 18), Cambridge, Ely Cathedral, Oxford (which he pronounced unique—August 6), Warwick, Kenilworth, Shrewsbury, Salisbury, Amesbury, jewel-like Wilton, (August 15), Portsmouth (including the Dock Yard), Chichester, and Stratford-on-Avon. In Shakespeare's quaint little town, Dana recorded: "I keep springing up in my chair and walking the room, clasping my hands together, and exclaiming upon my happiness, and what I had done, what cause was there that I should have it all within my power and possession" (August 8).[3]

Dana was courteously, even lavishly, entertained in England by various persons of rank. He especially admired the Duchess of Sutherland for her sailing manner of walk, her commanding mien, and her tenderly expressive face (July 23). The Duke of Argyll was kind, and so were the Marquis of Lansdowne, Sir Henry Holland, and especially Sir William Heathcote of Hursley, at whose country seat Dana was a guest. Another attentive host was Cranworth, the Lord Chancellor, who helped Dana obtain a superb visitor's seat in the House of Lords and at whose home he was introduced to Thomas Babington Macaulay.

In addition, Dana watched Benjamin Disraeli in action and commented on his masterly satire and his cool deliberation (July 25). At Cambridge, Dana was regally treated by Sir John Cole-

ridge, the poet's nephew and—what was more, to Dana—a vener-
able English judge of the assizes and a friend of England's Lord
Chief Justice Campbell, whom Dana also met. He talked famil-
iarly with many other celebrities, and was thrilled by everything
and everyone he saw in England, except perhaps certain fellow
Americans. He saw Queen Victoria and Prince Albert reviewing
troops at Aldershot on July 30; then two weeks later she happened to pass through Salisbury while Dana was there. He
thought her kind, matronly, and sensible, but not handsome
(August 15).

Knowing that he could not stay long in Paris, Dana sailed
across the Channel (proud that he was not seasick) for a brief
round of furious sight-seeing. On the way to his hotel, he quickly
sampled the best street sights in Paris—the Madeleine Church,
the Place de la Concorde, the Champs Élysées, the Tuileries, and
the Arc de Triomphe. Then, guidebook in hand, he hurried on
to the main points of interest in Paris. Among many other spots,
he saw the magnificent, endless Louvre; the Place Vendôme;
Notre Dame, which he called overloaded but impressive; the
Hôtel de Ville; the Morgue; "gorgeous" Sainte Chapelle; the site
of the Bastille; the Quai d'Orsay; the Palais Luxembourg; the
Palais de Justice; and, of course, innumerable glittering streets
and boulevards. He was pleased by a performance of a Molière
play at the Théâtre Français, by Franconi's, and by the perfect
manners of French grisettes and waiters (August 20, 21).

His last day in France he spent at Versailles, clucking Calvin-
istically at monarchical luxury displayed there at the palace, and,
beyond, at the Grand Trianon and the Petite Trianon. He quickly
returned to Paris, caught the evening boat-train for London
again, and concluded—on the basis of a fifty-eight-hour visit—
as follows about France: "Such as it is, with all the concealments
and gildings over of the crime there is known to be, and the
poverty there must be, with all its religion, showy or earnest, its
irreligion open or concealed, its science, its arts, its taste, its
politeness, its splendid civilization—I am thankful for the few
hours I have been able to spend in it, and for the new ideas and
new pictures it will furnish me for life" (August 21).[4]

Soon, too soon after that to suit him, Dana also took leave of
London—"London which has been to me a new world"—and then
of England: "Took my last look of the green shores of old En-

gland, her dear towers and trees, her cottages and village spires, the homes of so much of great and good, of honest and kind,— England, the salt of the earth" (August 23).[5] On the return voyage, Dana was manifestly proud of being one of the few passengers who were not seasick. He also narrowly observed the idle but busy social life of his fellow travelers. Distressed that steam was making the wind itself obsolete, Dana steamed into New York and was still American enough to appreciate Manhattan's matchless bay.

But he could now more intelligently balance the New World and the Old. "Here is a bright, piercing sun and clear sky, and all nerves set to concert pitch. There, across the water, in old England, is a mild sky, a mild sun, repose and quiet tints. There is maturity, fruition, and the culmination of civilization. Here is youth, hope, progress and earnest action. In two short months I have seen both. It is something in that brief time to have known two worlds" (September 3).[6]

Dana did not realize it at the time, but when he returned to hard work late in 1856, it was the beginning of the end of his career, compared to what it might have become with better luck. He was pleased that John Charles Frémont, the first Republican presidential candidate, polled in 1856 such an impressive victory for the party in Massachusetts that Republicans began for the first time to control the state. But Dana deplored the compromises and wire-pulling which necessarily preceded this triumph. Even more he was saddened by his precarious finances, which made it impossible for him to run as Republican candidate for the House of Representatives in Washington.

Shapiro expertly sums up the reasons for Dana's political eclipse: his Republican colleagues were "willing to recognize the necessities of practical politics, to engage in coalitions and to accept the support of men whose ideals were not in absolute accordance with their own. Dana's stiff rectitude and unbending code earned him a reputation as an unrealistic and unreliable dreamer, useful as a showpiece but not to be trusted with any real political power. Educated gentlemen like Dana still got elected to office . . . but their numbers and influence had sadly declined since the days of Federalist and Whig supremacy."[7]

Increased office and court work also curtailed Dana's lecturing and private writing. As Adams says, "It was during these years,

—the comparatively brief period between 1856 and 1860,—that Dana's practice was largest and most absorbing. His forensic reputation then stood at its height. A harder life than he lived during those years, or one better calculated to develop any lurking weak centre in the physical or nervous system it would have been difficult to devise." Detailing Dana's diabolical self-imposed regimen, Adams concludes that "The routine of his life during those years was as simple as it was killing."[8] Dana regularly rushed early from his Cambridge home by streetcar to his Boston office, drudged all morning there, wolfed an unsavory cafe lunch or forgot his midday meal entirely, then dashed back to his office or into court and worked until early evening. Then he had tea at home, studied his notes for the next day's work, then dined at eight. He often went over more papers until the wee hours.

Three of his most celebrated cases, upon which he expended his energies at this time, were hardly the sort that he would happily have dreamed of in law school. First he defended the Reverend Isaac S. Kalloch of Boston, charged with adultery. Dana's ingenuity resulted in a hung jury, after which the state agreed to drop proceedings when Kalloch promised to leave Massachusetts. Learning that the state had turned to other matters, the energetic minister gleefully confessed his guilt to Dana and refused to budge. Later, however, he migrated to San Francisco and became mayor of that tolerant metropolis.[9]

Next Dana expended great cleverness and got Benjamin F. Dalton off with a five-month sentence for murdering his wife's lover. When Dalton, visited in jail by his temporarily repentant mate, noticed that she was pregnant, his animosity was again aroused; and he retained Dana once more, this time to conduct his suit for divorce. Dana closed the case with a sixty-six-thousand-word summation delivered during parts of three days for a total of twelve cruel hours. In spite of the fact that Rufus Choate, the woman's lawyer, and evidently the judge himself opposed him eloquently, Dana had the satisfaction of hearing that ten jurors voted for his client and one of the two dissentients said he would also if the other would.

Perhaps Dana's most curious maritime case was that of *Seccomb v. Provincial Insurance Company*, a case that began in 1857 and lasted a decade. A legal nicety involved the geographical question of whether Smyrna (Izmir) was in Europe or in

Asia. A certain vessel was insured while it was in the Mediterranean and was going to ports in Europe. Taking a side trip to Smyrna, the hapless craft sank; and the ship owners, with the redoubtable Choate as attorney, defined Smyrna as in Europe, while Dana and the insurance company mapped Asia so as to include that city. After six trials, Dana's firm won the case, in spite of sympathy from various quarters for the plaintiff.

II *To Cuba and Back*

On February 11, 1859, Dana had a chance to take a brief vacation between court sessions. He did not want anyone to know about his freedom or his seeming means; so, saying goodbye to his family, he quietly caught a train to New York and on February 12 boarded the steamer *Cahawba* for Havana. He wanted a restful vacation of three weeks or so, but temperamentally he was unsuited for relaxation. Before arriving in Cuba, he had taken notes of enough details of the snowy coastline, steamship processes, the ship's captain and crew and passengers, changing climates at sea, the approach to Cuba, and the like, to wear out an ordinary mortal. Reluctant one night to leave the deck for the "sleeping-shelf" in his stateroom, he apologetically wrote as follows: "But there must be sleep for infirm human nature,—a nature that has even less self-sustaining power than a locomotive engine, and must not only be supplied with fuel and water at every stopping place, but must lie by, in a dark corner, in absolute repose and mere oblivion, for one quarter of its time, or it will wear out in a few days" (18-19).*

Once in Cuba, he set himself an almost killing pace. He spent his first four days in Havana in noting the filthiness of his hotel; comparing Americans, Spaniards, Cubans, Negroes, and coolies; attending mass at the Cathedral and the opera at the Teatro de Villanueva; and formally discussing in French the knotty problem of John Slidell's curious "Thirty Millions Bill" (for the purchase of Cuba by the United States) with the Bishop of Havana and several other high-ranking ecclesiasts.

The high point of Dana's stay in Cuba was his four-day ob-

---

* The parenthetical page references in this section are to Richard Henry Dana, Jr., *To Cuba and Back: A Vacation Voyage* (Boston, 1859).

servation of plantation life on a sugar *ingenio* at Limonar, near the port town of Matanzas. As the guest of Don Juan Chartrand and his family, Free Soiler Dana surprisingly sympathized with the owners rather than with the slaves; and he quoted approvingly the opinion of the New England-born engineer of the establishment: "this plantation is a favorable specimen, both for skill and humanity, and is managed on principles of science and justice, and yields a large return" (13). During the sugar season, Chartrand's Negro slaves slept six hours a night, had a total of an hour and a half for meals, and worked the rest of the time, whereas slave life on other plantations was worse. Then Dana adds that ". . . nursing mothers [owned by Chartrand] have lighter duties and frequent intervals of rest" (131).

The Yankee engineer reckoned plantation profits in 1859 at between 15 and 25 per cent on the investment. Dana showed a combination of self-deception and naïveté: he took seriously the Chartrands' statement that they disliked slavery but felt that the economic system required its temporary continuance;[10] and he was moved when he saw the slaves' children kneel before him and turn up to him "their simple, trusting faces" (14).

Free Soiler though he was, Dana probably restrained his criticism of Cuban slavery since he was a foreigner in Cuba and a guest of an aristocratic Spanish family at Limonar. He writes: "The only moral I am entitled to draw . . . is, that a well-ordered private house with slave labor, may be more neat and creditable than an ill-ordered public house with free labor. . . . I realize that I am far away in the hill country of Cuba, the guest of a planter, under this strange system, by which one man is enthroned in the labor of another race, brought from across the sea" (141).

Dana returned to Havana via Matanzas, where for a couple of days he saw such sights as the mountain of Cumbre and Yumurí Valley. On February 28, back in Havana, he called on more persons; attended mass at the Belen, where he wept at the "Tantum ergo Sacramentum"; and inspected the Military Hospital, the hospital of San Juan de Dios, and—with Samuel Gridley Howe—the horrible prison of Havana, called the Presidio. Next he dutifully attended a bullfight, knowing that he would not be pleased but feeling that he owed it to his education to go. His response was like that of many an honest American at a bullfight in Spain,

Mexico, Cuba, or North Africa—one of undisguised disgust. He was soon applauding the bull!

After attending a slave sale at the Regla, washing himself one last time in the rock-hewn sea-baths past the Paseo, and finally gathering all his notes and souvenirs, Dana boarded the *Cahawba* and left on March 2. He had spent twelve memorable days on Cuban soil. Death was with him on the voyage home, for the body of a former Louisiana chief justice had been put aboard for shipment to Massachusetts and burial there. Also a certain tubercular Mr. G—— was carried aboard more dead than alive; though he hoped to live to see New York again, he died a few hours before the steamer put in at that city, on March 7.

For reasons best known to himself, Dana returned instantly to arduous office work and yet found time at once to paste together a fifty-thousand-word account of his "vacation," which he called *To Cuba and Back: A Vacation Voyage*. Unbelievably, it was in print within two months after his return to Boston; and it quickly established itself as a reliable and sprightly Yankee reaction to things Cuban. Almost twenty editions of *To Cuba and Back* were published in the nineteenth century. Speaking of Dana and his rush to see everything in Cuba, Professor Hart rightly says that "If this furious sight-seeing does not go toward making a good literary production, it does make for an incisive and interesting account of Cuba at that time. He does not merely list tabulate and catalogue, but manages in his brief stay to give a very complete picture of the philosophic and sociological background of Cuba."[11] A lawyer and an observer of the political scene, Dana knew that Cuba in 1859 was important, as it was a century later and still is. Something of the tenseness concerning Cuba in the 1850's still vibrates in Dana's spotty but honest little book.

III *Around the World*

It should not be surprising that within a few months Dana was again perilously close to complete exhaustion. On July 20 he wrote in his *Journal*:

> I have overworked for the last ten years, undertaking to do everything and study everything. One day, a few weeks since, in the midst of arguing an exciting cause,—the "Smyrna

Case" (Seccomb *v*. Prov. Inc. Co.), I went into Parker's restaurant, and, very hungry, I ate, hardly knowing what I did, a quantity of cold corned beef, and returned into court, and finished my argument, and went back to Parker's to dine. While at dinner I was taken with a fit, from indigestion, and fell, senseless. I was taken to a bed, and a physician gave me an emetic. As soon as I was relieved I felt perfectly well. Most fortunately, there was no other result than a temporary fit,—nothing in the nature of paralysis.[12]

His physician said that a voyage around the world would be the best medicine, and Dana seemed to agree—at least his *Journal* says as much. But, at the same time, he hated the prospect of a year or more of enforced leisure.[13]

He kept a meticulous journal of his voyage around the world in the form of carefully written sheets which he periodically sent home to his wife and children. So it is easy—and delightful—to reconstruct his long, colorful, and adventure-filled trip.

He left New York late in July, 1859, on what he called a filthy ship bound for Havana and then for torrid Aspinwall, Panama. He crossed the Isthmus by train and thus traversed a continent on his birthday (August 1).* By mid-August he was back, by means of a clean ship, on California soil, for a pleasant four weeks which he detailed in his 1869 edition of *Two Years Before the Mast,* in an afterword entitled "Twenty-Four Years Later." This visit to California reinforced a feeling that Dana had expressed during a watery vacation in New Hampshire when he wrote to his wife on September 3, 1854: "I believe I was made for the sea, and that all my life on shore is a mistake. I was intended by nature for a general roamer and a traveller by sea and land, with occasional edits of narratives, and my duties as lawyer, scholar and publicist are all out of the way."[14]

Dana found many old faces and many changed places. He met Captain John Wilson, formerly of the sleek *Ayacucho,* and noted with pleasure that the good man was a rich and respected ranchero (August 20). He saw Alfred Robinson, the company agent whom he had not much liked earlier, and other former associates; and he learned the fate of still more of them. San Francisco was utterly different. Since the advent of the Vigilantes,

---

* Dates in parentheses in this section refer to entries in Dana's *Journal.*

it showed fewer signs of sin than New York (September 7). Los Angeles, too, was thriving and prosperous (August 22). On the other hand, Monterey was off the paths to gold mines and rivers, and hence was slipping commercially. San Diego was still Mexican. Many landmarks, which Dana had regarded as pleasantly permanent, had been swept away by the rush of progress. However, his memories of them remained strong:

> The past was real. The present, all about me, was unreal, unnatural, repellant. I saw the big ships lying in the stream, the *Alert,* the *California,* the *Rosa,* with her Italians; then the handsome *Ayacucho,* my favorite; the poor dear old *Pilgrim,* the home of hardship and hopelessness; the boats passing to and fro; the cries of the sailors at the capstan or falls; the peopled beach; the large hide-houses, with their gangs of men; and the Kanakas interspersed everywhere. All, all were gone! not a vestige to mark where one hide-house stood. The oven, too, was gone. I searched for its site, and found, where I thought it should be, a few broken bricks and bits of mortar. I alone was left of all, and how strangely was I here! What changes to me! Where were they all? . . .[15]

Dana of course knew that he was romanticizing even while he continued to do so: "How softening is the effect of time! It touches us through the affections. I almost feel as if I were lamenting the passing away of something loved and dear,—the boats, the Kanakas, the hides, my old shipmates! Death, change, distance, lend them a character which makes them quite another thing from the vulgar, wearisome toil of uninteresting, forced manual labor."[16] Leaving the Mission of San Diego, Dana turned his rented horse back to the steamer which was waiting for him, then paused to wave it all a farewell: "A last look—yes, last for life—to the beach, the hills, the low point, the distant town . . ."[17]

Then Dana took a vigorous ten-day plunge into the interior of California, traveling by rugged pack-trails along the Sierra Nevada Mountains and the Merced River to Stockton and Yosemite Valley, and thence all the way to John Charles Frémont's mills at his Rancho de las Mariposas, where he noted that the vigorous colonel's courage and resolution won over every obstacle (September 5).

When he boarded the *Mastiff,* commanded by one Captain Johnston and bound for Hawaii and then Hong Kong, Dana greatly relished this McKay clipper. But the ill-starred vessel caught fire at sea on September 15. Fortunately, the British steamer *Achilles* was a few miles astern, and within two hectic hours all aboard the clipper—including the few regular passengers and 175 Chinese in steerage—were saved, except for one Chinese who rashly dashed below after his money-box and was suffocated by the roiling smoke. Captain Johnston saved most of the passengers' luggage, some seventy-six thousand dollars in gold, and several of his flock of pets; but none of his own possessions or those of his bride were saved. During this wild adventure, Dana displayed calm courage by commanding one leaky lifeboat for a couple of extra trips to the steamer and by helping in many other ways to prevent panic. When the British captain landed the survivors in Honolulu and then sued for half the gold plus incidentals—totaling eighty-three thousand dollars—as legitimate salvage, maritime lawyer Dana was able to advise Johnston and reduce the claim against him to a mere eighty-three hundred dollars.

Dana had ample time to present innumerable letters of introduction to persons of authority in commercial and religious institutions, as he did during the entire trip, and hence he got about the islands more efficiently. He also obtained a half-hour audience with King Hamehameha IV; and he observed the scenery, Hawaiian institutions, and the weather. Unlike his friend Herman Melville, author of *Typee* and *Omoo,* he was especially pleased to note the success of the missionaries, both Catholic and Protestant, in their efforts to Christianize the islands.

Early in December Dana was back in San Francisco after almost four agonizingly tiresome weeks at sea. The inefficient backtracking tried his patience severely (November 16). But he made good use of a final month in California by visiting the Navy Yard at Mare Island overnight, nearby Vallejo, and the lush Napa Valley as a guest at the ranch of the legendary Indian fighter George C. Yount (December 26). Dana even took a stagecoach from San Francisco to see San Mateo and Alcatraz, Santa Clara, Alviso, and San José, from which city he visited the nearby quicksilver mines. After returning to San Francisco, where he rested over New Year's Eve and for a couple of days thereafter, he took a steamer to Sacramento for a week or so, during which he cannily observed the politicoes at the capital.

Then he again exchanged bustling activity on land for slow-paced ennui aboard the little *Early Bird,* as she took fifty-five days to sail to Hong Kong. Passengers included 230 Chinese in steerage, about whose safety Dana wondered since there were only three small lifeboats on the bark, two of which he professionally feared were leaky because of disuse (January 22, 1860). No misfortune occurred, and by mid-March, 1860, Dana was in Hong Kong. He quickly went on to swarming Canton, which, he noted, foreigners had not been able to see before the English and French military occupation of it only two years before.

He greatly admired Chinese industriousness: "In the shops are silk-weavers, wood-carvers, ivory-cutters and carvers, seal-cutters, spinners, lacquer-workers,—an ant-hill of industry! Everything done by hand and nothing by machinery. You might as well introduce steam into an ant-hill as into China. What would become of the three hundred million workers, each making the ninth part of the pin, and each getting enough to eat and clothe himself?" (March 11).[18]

Dana exhibited insatiable curiosity in China. He studied Chinese religious habits, domestic and eating habits, buildings and streets, schools and colleges, legal institutions, hospitals, cemeteries, and natural scenery. He went briefly to Macao, and even boarded a few British gunboats in the harbor. Then early in April he went by way of Shanghai on to Nagasaki, Yokohama, "Fusiyama," and Hakodadi, among other places, in a three-week tour of Japan. He admired the Japanese children, deplored the older women's habit of blackening their teeth, admired delicate colored drawings of birds (saying that a country which produced artists of such ability must be called "civilized"—April 26), walked aghast into and through brothels, and braved certain half-deserted Kenegawa streets at night, armed with revolver and bowie knife. When told that he had been foolish, he agreed but noted tolerantly that it must have been annoying to the Japanese to admit Westerners reluctantly and then have to provide them police protection (April 19).

After a brief return to Shanghai and then Hong Kong, he took a cruise among the Chusan islands and visited a few spots on the Chinese mainland. Then he was at sea again, homeward-bound (June 9). In less than two weeks he was recording his preference for the beauty of Penang, the little British island off the west

85

coast of the Malay Peninsula, over any other spot in the Far East. He sought out the neatly marked grave of a college chum of his who had died there of fever contracted on Sumatra: "This was [he noted], perhaps, the most interesting incident of my travels in the East, the more so from its being unexpected. . . . I plucked some grass and leaves which were growing on the grave, to take home . . . I am glad, too, to get rid of the associations I had with Penang,—of deadly fevers, miasmas, Malays, and low, damp soil, and to see his grave amid so much beauty of nature and so much care of art" (June 18).[19]

Next, dreamy, aromatic Ceylon, then Bombay, where he recorded that his heart sank at the news of Abraham Lincoln's nomination, rather than that of William H. Seward (June 25). Poor Dana was in pain enough at this time from a broken rib, caused when the storm-lashed ship carrying him to India pitched and threw him across the deck and into a stanchion. (Earlier, he had broken his left little toe during a fall on horseback when a suspension bridge had collapsed over the Wailuku River in Hawaii.) The injured rib cost him three extra weeks in Bombay, but he noted in his *Journal* that patience amid blessings was not particularly virtuous (July 6). He visited the garrison city of Poona, 130 miles by train from Bombay. He was intrigued by simply watching the swarms of people of many races, castes, nationalities, and social strata, downtown in vivid Bombay (July 21). As usual, Dana also visited churches, schools, and all the well-to-do local merchants he could find; and he took notes on everything which passed his vision.

Late in July he took a steamer for Aden, which he visited for only part of a day (August 4). By August 10 he had steamed up the Red Sea, seen Africa for the first time, and cast anchor at Suez at an awkward midsummer date. The landscape was oppressively dreary (August 11). From Cairo, to which a desert train transported him over miles of sand, he went to the silent Pyramids and the disappointing Sphinx by donkey—"Donkeys, donkeys everywhere, and camels! There are Joseph's brethren, ambling down the street, each riding his ass . . . " (August 12).[20] Perhaps the closest Dana came to betraying fatigue is in the following entry: "It is now sundown, and here, in this dreary, magnificent spot, I am to pass the night. My dragoman makes me up a bed of blankets and my mat on the hard stone forming the lower range of the pyramid. . . . Once in the night I awoke. Stars and moon bright,—sky cloudless and the Arabs lying in the sand; but the pyramid recedes too fast for me to see the top, where I lie" (August 13).[21] After coffee and bread at four in the morning, Dana was refreshed enough to climb to the top of Cheops, "a few minutes before sunrise, and have the great gratification of seeing from the top of the highest pyramid the blood-red African sun rise over this vast expanse,—this expanse, now of sand and water, of scattered villages, the illimitable Libyan desert on the west, and glittering in the east the citadel of Cairo" (August 14),[22] where he saw everything sumptuous and decorative in two hectic days before moving on again. As he proceeded by train to Alexandria, the Nile Delta reminded him of rich Connecticut River bottomland.

Chanting Byron, Dana found his spirits reviving as he threaded his way by steamer through the isles of Greece. "The Peloponessus!" "Here is Navarino Bay!" And of Corfu, "What a romantic and beautiful spot!" (August 20, 21).[23] Then Trieste at last: "I am in Europe! It is an exciting thought, and one calling for gratitude. I have been carried across the Pacific, through all the seas, and inland journeys and changes of climate, and heats and dangers of China and Japan, and of the eastern seas and British India and Egypt, without so much as a hair of my head injured" (August 23).[24] (But a toe and a rib had been broken.)

He evidently made a puritanical vow to spend only a single day in Venice, but he stayed there for three fascinating days: "It took me as much by surprise as if I had never heard of it. . . . People may be divided into two classes, those who have seen Venice and can believe in the actualizing of the imagination, and those who have not seen it, and may not so believe" (August 23);[25] it was "the most interesting and incredible creation of man's hands in the form of town or city on the Earth's surface!" (August 27).[26] Nonetheless, he also regarded Venice as a vicious oligarchy.

He cut by train across northern Italy to Milan, finding its cathedral almost indescribable. A series of diligences then took him north and into Switzerland: "Nothing in America is to be compared with the Alps. All the mountains in New Hampshire might be taken from a single range of the Alps and not be missed" (August 29).[27] By the first of September he had worked his way

87

to "charming" Geneva. At this point Dana must have begun to feel somewhat guilty, uneasy at selfishly spending so much time and money and energy, at gratifying himself while his family remained at home. So he began to hurry. September 6 found him off the Rhine and leaving Cologne for Antwerp, and the next day he caught a steamer for London. "Here I am, in dear old London again!" (September 8), where for the first time in months he was able to pick up mail from home; ". . . and when I found all well,—all living,—it seemed that my cup of blessing was full" (September 8).[28]

He devoted a scant week to England this time, and found everything richly pleasing, from Hyde Park to York Minster to Lincoln Cathedral, which Macaulay had recommended in 1856 as a unique delight. He spent almost no time visiting London friends in out-of-season September—his wardrobe was also unsuitable, he noted (September 11)—but instead rested and prepared for the Atlantic crossing. In mid-September he took a steamer carrying 180 passengers (mostly quite commonplace, he noted—September 16) to New York, where he docked a dozen days later. On September 27 he penned the following terse summary in his *Journal*: "This day opens in America—home. Been absent 433 days, of which spent about 233 on the water and 200 on land. New York completes the circumnavigation of the globe!"[29]

The entire adventure, like his briefer trips to England, to France, and to Cuba, filled his retentive mind with a multitude of shimmering images which he never forgot; and it must have done him a world of good physically. But the America to which he now returned had also been on the move, and poor Dana soon found that he had not kept up with its progress as faithfully as he had recorded his own in notes and letters.

CHAPTER 5

Storm Clouds, 1861-1882

BEFORE HIS SICKNESS in 1859, which necessitated his absence from home, Dana had met his reverses with positive success; and his popularity after the Massachusetts Constitutional Convention and the Burns case was high. But, from the time of his return to Boston late in 1860 until his death, his life was pathetic; his few triumphs were clouded by misfortunes.

I *Lincoln's District Attorney*

With his typically unfortunate timing, Dana was still on his tour around the world during most of the presidential campaign of 1860. When he returned to the United States, therefore, he was somewhat confused by the complicated issues on the eve of the first national victory for the Republican party and by the inexorable approach of the Civil War. If he had been home stumping for Abraham Lincoln, he might have deserved a share of the spoils which began to shower upon his friends in the fall. As it was, Senator Charles Sumner and Charles Francis Adams, then a Representative from Massachusetts, had all they could do to wangle an appointment for him as President Lincoln's United States Attorney for the District of Massachusetts.

And two less harmonious supporting pillars Dana could hardly have chosen than Adams and Sumner. Adams had been favoring a policy of conciliation toward the South to gain time for Lincoln between election and inauguration; but Sumner, who could never forget the cruel caning given him in 1856 by Preston Brooks, was adamant in regarding Southerners as simply rebels. Sumner and Adams supported Dana even as he balanced their irreconcilable positions before their very noses. By a freak of fate, Dana's nomination went to the Senate on April 12, 1861, the day Fort Sumter was fired on.

The Civil War altered the function of a federal district attorney. Dana might have preferred a consular appointment, but he hurled himself with characteristic energy into his new office. He proceeded vigorously against inhumane sea captains and those illegally trafficking in African slaves, and against bounty-jumpers, draft-dodgers, and liquor-tax evaders. But his most spectacular service involved the so-called prize cases.

When Confederate ships ran afoul of the blockade, which was one of Lincoln's most effective weapons, their Yankee captors took them to their home ports as war loot for the Union. At first Boston was so far from the scene of action that it had few cases, but it was not long before Dana had gained the reputation of being fast and fair. Therefore he soon had far more than his share of admiralty work on his desk. As Shapiro helpfully summarizes the matter,

> Following the proceedings suggested in Justice Story's volume on Prize Law and the precedents laid down by Lord Stowell during the Napoleonic wars, Dana worked out a speedy and effective system for dealing with vessels brought into his jurisdiction. He had the United States Marshal for the district hold the ship and sell it at auction as soon as possible, while elaborate depositions were taken from every member of the captured crew. Vessels disposed of in this way were often bought by the government and played an important part in the rapid expansion of the Navy. Proceedings *in rem* against the money realized from the sale were rapid and almost always successful; sometimes Dana was able to distribute prize shares to the captors within sixty days after a vessel arrived in port.[1]

If the whole business was profitable to the North, it was proportionately so to Dana. Above his annual salary of six thousand dollars he was entitled by a law passed in 1862 to six thousand dollars more in fees; then, when he legally represented the interested parties which had captured the prizes, he took in as much more as twelve hundred dollars for each seized ship. As though this were not enough, he occasionally commanded thousand-dollar retainers to conduct appeals, and he was also permitted to pursue private practice in odd moments. Shapiro estimates that Dana's wartime income exceeded twenty thousand dollars annually, enough to permit him to pay off all debts, renovate his house, and indulge in some land speculation.[2]

Establishing the legality of seizing blockade runners trying to enter Confederate ports at a time when war had not been declared against the South taxed even Dana's brilliant legal mind. Shapiro succinctly writes that "as Sumner pointed out to Dana early in the conflict, 'prize [law] is essentially *jure belli,*' and to use it against Confederate shipping implied the existence of a war and the validity of the secession ordinances. If the government admitted the existence of a war then it could not legitimately deny beligerent status to the Confederacy or its right to seek help from foreign powers."[3]

Dana extricated Lincoln from this tangle by his inspired handling of the *Amy Warwick* case. The *Amy Warwick,* a ship owned by three men living in Richmond, Virginia, was seized in July, 1861, on its way from Rio de Janeiro to New York carrying one hundred and sixty thousand dollars worth of coffee. The government's case was not impressive: the *Amy Warwick* had been bound for the friendly port of New York; two of her owners were Unionists; and part of the non-belligerent cargo of coffee was owned by Londoners. But Dana had the ship condemned in Boston on the grounds that her owners were residents of a rebel state and that her cargo would put money into rebel pockets.

By December, 1862, a number of prize-case appeals had been taken to the Supreme Court, which a month before had been thoughtfully packed by Lincoln with three new and sensible judges. So his Attorney-General, Edward Bates, asked the Supreme Court to hear the appeals in one block. Knowing that Lincoln's government would be on trial in the eyes of the world, Bates called to his side the country's best lawyers, including Dana's old law-school chum William H. Evarts. Dana offered to go to Washington and argue the case without fee. Bates agreed but later paid him one thousand dollars for his services,[4] which —in the words of one historian—"probably saved the government from defeat that would have been catastrophic."[5]

Dana argued flawlessly, and he confined himself to the question of enemy property. If coffee seized at sea belonged to persons living behind enemy lines, it was fair to take it and thus keep the enemy from gaining by it. But who was the enemy? Dana argued that an insurrection rather than a *de jure* war was in process and that Lincoln, even without Congressional support, had every right to seize cargo at sea to weaken the power of the insurrectionists. If the cargo happened to be owned by loyalists living among the rebels, that was simply an unfortunate circumstance and those loyalists were innocent victims. Lincoln, as commander-in-chief of the United States in time of insurrection, might if necessary hang rebellious traitors and even set aside the constitutional rights of innocent loyalists everywhere.

Agreeable though the nine judges were to Dana's reasoning that the President could seize cargo at sea which might aid the rebel cause, only five judges accepted his arguments extending the commander-in-chief's power during an insurrection. But all nine judges were impressed by Dana's logic and eloquence. An eyewitness of the Supreme Court arguments was agog at what he called Dana's

> . . . luminous and exquisite presentation of the status which armed the Executive with power to use the methods and processes of war to suppress the great rebellion. Dry legal questions were lifted into the higher region of international discussion, and the philosophy of the barbaric right of capture of private property at sea was for the first time in the hearing of most of the judges then on the bench applied to the pending situation with a power of reasoning and a wealth of illustration and a grace and felicity of style that swept all before them. After Mr. Dana had closed his argument, I happened to encounter Judge Grier [Democrat Robert C. Grier of Pennsylvania], who had retired for a moment to the corridor in the rear of the bench, and whose clear judicial mind and finely cultivated literary taste had keenly enjoyed the speech, and, in a burst of unjudicial enthusiasm, he said to me, "Well, your little 'Two Years Before the Mast' has settled that question; there is nothing more to say about it!"[6]

Lincoln was evidently also much impressed by Dana, who wrote home in 1864: "The President told me he had read my pamphlet on the decision of the Supreme Court, and that it cleared up his mind on the subject entirely; that it reasoned out and put into scientific statement what he had all along felt in his bones must be the truth of the matter, and was not able to find anywhere in the books, or to reason out satisfactorily himself."[7]

92

On his side, Dana changed his attitude toward Lincoln. Dana had had serious and deep misgivings about Lincoln, whom he regarded in 1862 as a kind of commercial drummer in the White House and, a year later, as "an utterable calamity to us where he is," although he had "a kind of shrewdness and common sense, mother wit, and slipshod, low levelled honesty."[8] After Lincoln had praised him for his work in the prize cases, Dana could honestly return the compliment, if with continued reservations; and he wrote his father:

> Such a shapeless mass of writhing ugliness as slouched about in the President's chair, you never saw or imagined; & you form & discard several opinions of him in half an hour. He is an anomaly. You can't help feeling interested in him & a sympathy for him. You value his good & strong points, and fear his weak points will wreck him or wreck something.
>
> I think the soundest opinion of him is this—He is good at coming to a sound & adequate understanding of a large question, and at explaining his results popularly when he has reached them; but lacks administrative power & discrimination of individuals, & yields too easily to personal influence in matters of administration respecting individuals.[9]

Of Lincoln's assassination, Dana wrote his schoolboy son that "It is the most frightful tragedy in history." He added, "I had come to know Mr. Lincoln well. I believe he had come to like & respect me. I heard of several things he said which showed how he felt towards me. The last time I saw him, he put his arms round me, as if he had been my father, and seemed to want to keep me. His re-election, and the confidence the country placed in him, make his a great loss. . . . These events make us all feel very solemn,— even gloomy."[10]

With the war ended, Lincoln dead, and his own services in Washington no longer necessary, Dana began to care less and less for the routine of his job as district attorney in Boston. He had missed a great opportunity in the fall of 1861 when Congressman William Appleton from Dana's Fifth District of Massachusetts resigned because of poor health. Dana had been urged by various powerful friends to seek the nomination, but he had felt that, if elected, he could not afford the position. And he had received no encouragement from his land-dabbling father, his rich aunts, or even his ensconced wife. So he had refused. Now, after the war, he coasted professionally for a time, retaining his title as district attorney and collecting his fees but letting his assistants do the office work until he officially resigned in September, 1866. By this time Dana had begun revising Henry Wheaton's classic work, *Elements of International Law*, at the request of the author's needy widow. A new and dramatic phase of Dana's life was soon to unfold.

II *Plagiarism*

Henry Wheaton, the sort of man Dana aspired to be, "combined the advantages of the discipline of a barrister, the culture of a scholar, the experiences of a diplomat, and the habits of a man of society. And it is no small thing to add, that, to a subject essentially moral, he brough a purity of nature, candor, and fidelity to truth and duty, as remarkable as his learning, industry, and philosophy."[11] These are Dana's own words, used to sum up the character of Henry Wheaton, a brilliant American lawyer, author, linguist, and diplomat in Europe from 1827 until two years before his death in 1848 at the age of sixty-three.

Wheaton had first published his internationally respected *Elements* in two 1836 editions and later in two more editions just before his death. Then a former friend of his named William Beach Lawrence, a wealthy Rhode Island Democratic lawyer, had set to work on a new edition published in 1855 by Little, Brown and Company of Boston, the publisher C. C. Little being Mrs. Wheaton's son-in-law. The advent of the Civil War made a new edition imperative, and Lawrence in 1863 came out with a long-winded and somewhat pro-Southern one, which displeased both Little and Mrs. Wheaton, and which Dana slurringly cited in his prize-case writings. Casting about for a better editor this time, Little first asked Charles Sumner, who refused, and then Dana, in whose offices Wheaton's son had once studied law. Dana declined late in 1863 but was finally persuaded to accept by his friend Mrs. Wheaton.[12]

Dana converted his Cambridge study into what he called "a work-shop and depot of international law."[13] He slaved unselfishly for two years on his magnificent monographic notes for the edition, writing more than 250 of them in all—some very brief but others as long as twenty pages each. He considered in these essay-notes such matters as the Monroe Doctrine, belligerency in civil wars, prize jurisdiction, the carrying of hostile persons and papers on neutral ships, and other subjects. His edition of Wheaton's *Elements* was considered in 1936 to be valuable enough to deserve republication through the Carnegie Endowment for International Peace in Washington. In the words of George Grafton Wilson, a distinguished professor of law, "Dana's edition of Wheaton's *International Law* came to be recognized as one of the leading authorities cited in the courts of the world during the nineteenth century."[14]

William Beach Lawrence, the ousted editor, did not concur in any praise of Dana by anyone. Three months after the new edition was published in July, 1866, he began a suit against Dana for plagiarism. The resulting case dragged through the courts for the next thirteen years, and the affair greatly depressed Dana. The controversy is a complex and unpleasant story of wrong on both sides.[15]

Lawrence was a verbose editor who had been associated with Wheaton's *Elements* so long that he seemed to feel he had written the book. As editor, he even wanted his name above the author's on the title page. Arguing with Wheaton's widow, he vowed late in 1863 to have nothing more to do with her but instead to publish a new edition of Wheaton in Leipzig. At this point Dana innocently entered the scene; but Lawrence did not know of his rival's edition until shortly before it was scheduled to appear, whereupon he evidently threatened and raged at Dana, who was so offensively calm and superior that Lawrence vowed revenge. Soon the suit began.

Dana strode into court with his usual Boston Brahmin mien but hardly with clean hands. In his preface he had written that "This edition contains nothing but the text of Mr. Wheaton, according to his last revision, his notes, and the original matter contributed by the editor [Dana himself]"; and then still more pointedly he had stated that "The notes of Mr. Lawrence do not form any part of this edition."[16] This was a tactical blunder.

Under cross-examination by Lawrence's lawyer, Dana confessed to private mistakes as well. He was innocent of using notes which Lawrence had written, but he had cited and quoted some rare manuscript and newspaper material not only cited by

Lawrence in his notes but owned in America only by Lawrence and never personally read by Dana. Even more damaging was the revelation that he had reproduced a few errors of citation which his careless predecessor Lawrence was vengeful enough now to admit existed in his edition. Dana's best defense—and it was not quite good enough—was that by birth, education, and professional accomplishments, he was above reproach; that he was in the forefront among writers and lecturers on the subject of international law; that answering his adversary's specific charges in detail would involve too much expense in time and money; and that he had agreed to edit Wheaton's book simply to help out the man's widow.

Observing acidly that such a defense was at best vague, the judge decided in Lawrence's favor in September, 1869. But then the judge hedged: he refused to stop the sale of Dana's edition; he denied Lawrence exclusive control over subsequent editions of Wheaton; and, finally, declaring that Dana had indeed infringed Lawrence's rights by paralleling some annotated material, he referred the case to Henry W. Paine, master in chancery, to decide the degree of infringement.[17]

The ruling placed Dana in a miserable position. As Adams puts it, "he stood convicted of plagiarism and literary piracy, but with sentence deferred until the extent of his misdeeds should be definitely ascertained. It might amount to nothing at all, or it might amount to a great deal; but until, through the report of the Master, it should be definitely ascertained whether it was one or the other, he was exposed at any time to attacks almost impossible to meet."[18]

For a decade, while the meticulous Master Paine turned over the bulky depositions, Dana was under a cloud which prevented him from being seen, especially by important men in Washington, for what he was—a scholarly gentleman with a brilliant legal mind who ached to serve his country in some important capacity. When Paine filed his final report, it was too late: Dana was sixty-five years of age, had retired from all work but sporadic scholarship, and was pretty well worn out.

Paine privately opined that Dana "had in the Wheaton litigation been a victim of the bitterest and most unrelenting persecution he had ever known."[19] Publicly, Paine decreed that of 146 instances of alleged plagiarism only fourteen involved technical infringement under the judge's own definition. The monographic notes which Dana proudly pointed to as his own were shown not to have come in any way from Lawrence. But the vindication came too late: the damage had been done, nobody cared very much about the truth, and in addition Dana through the intervening decade had uniformly failed in other ways too.

III *Failures*

From 1867 until his retirement from the profession of law in 1878, nothing that Dana attempted to do turned out well. It was almost as though he were cursed; but perhaps he was simply too sophisticated for Reconstruction times.

He ran successfully for the Massachusetts Legislature in the fall of 1866, shortly after his plagiarism case had begun. He hoped that this position might lead to a federal legislative post. Refusing opulent law cases brought to his office, he worked hard as a state representative and during his second term became head of the Judiciary Committee and hence was the leader of the House. He successfully spoke in favor of repealing the outmoded usury law, saying that "no law should stand that cannot be enforced."[20] But his almost hypocritical position against repeal of prohibition of liquor reduced his popularity. Like many theoretical thinkers in the 1920's, he wanted prohibition laws on the books and a little medicinal whiskey in his own parlor. At one point he was fatally dubbed "the Duke of Cambridge." He sought no third term.

Meanwhile, in 1867 his friend William Evarts was ordered by President Andrew Johnson to institute civil prosecution of Confederate ex-President Jefferson Davis on a charge of treason. Evarts retained Dana as one of his assistants in this touchy case. To try Davis as a traitor would be unnecessarily bloodthirsty, especially since more than two years had passed since his arrest. To release him was apt to be politically suicidal since Davis was still hated by influential Northern hotheads and since President Johnson's ears were constantly ringing with the cry "Hang Jeff Davis!" And to aim at anything between execution and pardon might result in an embarrassing failure.

Dana was influential in persuading Evarts—soon to become Attorney-General after defending President Johnson during his impeachment—to delay Davis' trial and finally to free him entirely as part of the General Amnesty Act of Christmas, 1868. Dana's sound reasons for wanting to avoid trying Davis are cogently summarized by Richard Henry Dana, III:

> . . . he took the position, and so advised the government, that it was unwise to proceed, partly because it would be impossible to convict before a jury drawn from any of the scenes of Mr. Davis's overt acts, namely, the Confederate States, without excluding every man with secession sympathies, which in effect would look very like packing the jury with those of Northern feelings; while to try him in the North, for example in the State of Pennsylvania, on the ground that some of the troops of which he was the nominal commander-in-chief had invaded that state, would look very like changing the venue to secure conviction; that to punish one man, though a leader, and let others off who were as much if not more to blame for secession, would create a feeling of unfairness; and mainly, he took the broader ground that our policy should be to reunite the country into one lasting union, and for this, a magnanimous course of pardon was more effective than punishment. In this way, his advice was against his chance to increase a reputation which the trial of such a great national cause would have done.[21]

Dana was reviled for his part in these proceedings; however, history proves him to have been moderate and farsighted.

Conservative Republican Dana was resoundingly defeated in his bid for the House of Representatives in Washington by the notorious General Benjamin Franklin Butler, radical Republican incumbent from Essex County, Massachusetts, where neither man lived. The people kidded Dana for his fancy gloves and ducal manners, and cared not one whit for his intelligent comments on Butler's shady, turncoat past during the Civil War and on his present irresponsible Greenback and anti-Grant policies. Dana made at least two mistakes during his campaign: he lectured relentlessly on purely political issues; and, in portraying himself as a former hide-droghing seaman from the wilds of California, he seemed to be talking down to his audience of callous-handed Massachusetts fishing folk. Wild Ben Butler organized the police, fire department, local marching musicians, subordinate speakers, and even the press in a positive orgy of demagoguery.

When the votes were counted, Dana had eighteen hundred out of a total of twenty thousand cast.[22]

Having been absent from his office long enough in defending himself when called a plagiarist and in campaigning for Congress, he now returned to his practice and soon began to command colossal fees—for example, five thousand dollars in a legacy dispute and eight thousand dollars in a banking case.[23] But he continued to dream of political glory on a federal level and, better still, of diplomatic triumphs. He once wrote, "I shall not avoid any decent public duties that may come to me, for I have a conscience about American citizenship; but our politics look low and dark. They seem to be drifting off beyond the reach of the moral opinion of society."[24] He had naturally been disappointed when his friend Charles Francis Adams had been dispatched to Geneva to represent America in the 1871-72 arbitrations to settle the *Alabama* and related claims against England. Dana, pardonably prejudiced in his own favor, felt that his experience in the prize cases made him uniquely qualified; however, history shows that Adams did superlative work in Geneva.[25] As a sop, Dana was later sent to Halifax to represent the United States in conferences involving disputed fishing rights, which, along with boundary claims and the *Alabama* affair, were to be arbitrated under terms of the 1871 Treaty of Washington.

But first Dana had to undergo the saddest reverse of his life. It was bitterer than Lawrence's attack on his honor and more humiliating than Butler's destruction of his political ambition; and it grew out of both men's enmity toward him.

One of the most sensational scandals to occur during President Ulysses S. Grant's administration involved Robert C. Schenck, America's dishonest ambassador to England. While Schenck was escaping from London early in 1876, one jump ahead of the victims of his Utah silver-mine swindle, President Grant and Secretary of State Hamilton Fish, Dana's friend, cast about for an impeccable successor and fastened upon Dana. There must have been no happier moment in his life than when Dana received word in March that he had been formally nominated to become ambassador to England. He had often sought positions of honor and responsibility; but this offer came unsought, as a recognition of his illustrious family name, his past services to his country, his literary and social fame, and his personal worth. His mission to the glittering court of St. James would crown his career and set a standard for future ambassadors.

The press almost unanimously applauded President Grant's choice. Dana's friends deluged him with congratulations, of which the following from James Russell Lowell is representative:

> There are two places for which I have always thought you preeminently fit. One is the Massachusetts senatorship, & the other has just been offered you. . . . It is a strong witness to your powers as a disinfectant, that you should be expected not only to neutralize the malodorousness of Skunk [Robert C. Schenck], but to sweeten a mortifying administration. We need not be wholly cast down when nominations are still possible that are applauded on both sides the water.[26]

Many other important persons joined the chorus which sang Dana's praises. But within two weeks the opposition had gathered with tomahawks agleam. W. B. Lawrence rushed to Washington and testified to Democratic enemies of Dana that he was not only a plagiarist but also a perjurer anxious to rush off to England to escape court proceedings then in progress against him. Vindictive Ben Butler, though he privately admitted that the nomination was a sensible one and though he was not then a Congressman, rounded up all the anti-Dana Republican Senators he could get hold of.

Members of the Senate Foreign Relations Committee did not want to read a thousand pages or so of depositions having to do with plagiarism and other recondite literary technicalities; it was easier to accept Lawrence's distortion that Dana was a simple thief and liar. And smarting under Fish's tactless failure to consult them before announcing the appointment—the Secretary of State had merely sought to give Schenck time to get out of England in secret!—the majority of Senators sided with Butler. Many reporters and political friends rallied around Dana; but Simon Cameron, chairman of the Foreign Relations Committee, chose to believe Lawrence and Butler, and notified Fish that his choice was going to be rejected. Fish went to President Grant himself, who forced Cameron's committee to hold off long enough to give Dana a chance to appear before it in person.[27]

Dana then made another of his several proud and half-admirable mistakes. He demanded in an open telegram to Massachu-

setts Senator George S. Boutwell the right to appear before
Cameron's committee to clear away the mud Lawrence and
Butler had cast on his name. His friend Evarts wired his encouragement a day later: "I think I would go to Washington."[28]
But then Dana began to fear that Cameron's committee, already
poisoned by his enemies, would be nothing but another court
packed against him. So, unwilling as usual to take off his spotless
gloves and fight for an honor deservedly his and an appointment
to the advantage of his country, he fell back on his precious
family reputation and coolly sent off a controversial public letter
to Boutwell. Since it is of great importance in elucidating Dana's
curious personality, it should be quoted at some length:

> When I first heard that charges were to be made against
> me before the committee, my impulse was to demand a hear-
> ing, . . . but in my telegram . . . I said that if the question
> was upon my general fitness, I had nothing to say; but I
> could not believe that a committee would listen to charges
> affecting my honor from antagonists, and decide adversely
> to me, without offering some opportunity of explanation. . . .
> This morning I learn the facts authentically for the first time.
> I learn that the committee did give a secret *ex parte* hearing
> to two men known to be my enemies on personal grounds,
> and on that hearing alone came to an adverse decision and
> acted upon it. They had no intention of seeking information
> from me or my friends. . . . They . . . requested the Presi-
> dent to withdraw my nomination, with the understanding that
> if he did not they should report adversely. I understand that
> it is only upon the urgent request of persons entitled to their
> attention . . . that they have consented to let the matter lie
> over until Tuesday [March 21, 1876], that I may be heard
> if I wish to be. . . .
> I trust . . . that you know me well enough to know that I
> shall not ask to be heard before the committee under such
> circumstances. I value highly the honor of the office tendered
> to me, and am grateful to the government for the dis-
> tinguished compliment. When I saw the surprising unanim-
> ity, and I may even say enthusiasm, with which it was re-
> ceived by the press and the public,—altogether the most
> gratifying thing I ever experienced,—I will say to you frankly
> that it removed every doubt arising out of my private [finan-
> cial] circumstances, and that I determined to accept the
> office; but there is nothing in the gift of the government

> which would induce me to go to Washington and submit
> a question touching my honor to a committee which has
> taken the course which has been taken by the Senate Com-
> mittee on Foreign Relations. . . . If the Senate reject it [the
> nomination] under the present circumstances, I trust I shall
> not fail of the grace to submit with equanimity.[29]

From his point of view, Dana had behaved admirably. Many
of his friends applauded in their way, and President Grant
doggedly continued to support him. But Cameron's committee
was implacable. In retrospect, it is fair to say that Dana lost a
splendid chance to serve his country and himself by not con-
sidering John Milton's magnificent lines from "Areopagitica":
"I cannot praise a fugitive and cloistered virtue, unexercised and
unbreathed, that never sallies out and sees her adversary, but
slinks out of the race where the immortal garland is to be run
for, not without dust and heat."

Vilifying Dana as, among other things, "One of those damn
literary fellers," Cameron led all of his fellow Democratic Senators and several Republicans to reject his nomination on April
5, 1876. As Adams put it, "Had the nomination of Mr. Dana been
confirmed, there can be no doubt he would have held the English
mission, had he so desired, throughout the administration of
President Hayes [1877-81], who succeeded General Grant, in-
asmuch as his warm personal friend, Mr. Evarts, was then Secretary of State. It would have been an agreeable and fitting end of
Mr. Dana's active life; but . . . it was not to be."[30]

In June, 1876, Dana demonstrated his continuing patriotism
by going as a delegate-at-large to the Republican Convention
in Cincinnati and there—still true to his evil demon—backed the
wrong candidate. He officially seconded Benjamin H. Bristow,
but a majority of the delegates passed up both Bristow and the
more luminous James G. Blaine to name Rutherford B. Hayes. It
should not have been surprising, therefore, that nothing material-
ized when Dana, who admired but had only tardily supported
Hayes, sat back and waited blissfully for some sort of consular
plum to be aimed at his lap. Evarts offered Dana's son an un-
important legation secretaryship in which to loaf through a pro-
tracted honeymoon, since he knew that the young man was about
to marry Edith Longfellow, the poet's daughter whose "golden
hair" is celebrated in his popular "Children's Hour." Declining

such a transparent sop, Dana sat back and waited a little longer. It was June before he learned what his reward was to be: he could help represent President Hayes on the Fisheries Commission soon to convene at Halifax.

Once an inflammatory diplomatic and commercial topic, the dispute between Canada and the United States over fishing rights off the eastern shores of Canada now seems like nothing very exciting. But Dana characteristically threw himself into his homework, represented his government with all his old forensic skill, and lost the case. The final decision of the board in November was a shocking insult to the United States. However, it was not Dana's fault, since Ensign H. Kellogg, the American commissioner, for whom Dana was counsel, was evidently a sloppy, sleepy old man and was less than useless during the proceedings. Moreover, the canny British government had jockeyed a pro-British Belgian named Baron Maurice Delfosse onto the board as the "neutral" commissioner, and was in secret communication with the ostensibly impartial Canadian commissioner, Sir Alexander Galt. To quote the conclusion of Shapiro, who interestingly narrates the whole sorry fiasco, "All the available evidence makes it clear that Delfosse and Galt had not adhered to the limited, literal interpretation of the treaty upon which Dana had insisted during the hearings."[31]

Once again other forces had stacked the cards against Dana. For a while he hoped for other government work—perhaps an important elective position, possibly a consular appointment, or a cabinet post—but in his heart he knew, in fact he had known for some years, that his public life was at an end. In 1873 he had diagnosed his own case with the sure eye and hand of a master physician when he blamed his failure on lack of money and then himself for that lack:

> . . . my life has been a failure, compared with what I might and ought to have done. My great success—my book—was a boy's work, done before I came to the Bar. I was going on well in professional success, and I had made a great forensic success in the constitutional convention of 1853,— up to the time of my sickness and absence in 1859-1860. It was not so much overwork that broke me down,—that never hurt me,—as anxiety and care. . . . My talents and tastes fitted me especially for parliamentary life; and, when my

party came in, I could have probably gone to Congress, and I am sure I should have distinguished myself. But I had no money, and was obliged to refuse the offers of my friends. That was the career for me. I have no right to lay the fault wholly on the people or our institutions. I had my chance, and my want of means, which was my own fault,—certainly not the fault of the public,—precluded me. In my youth I thought it a fine thing to despise money, but forgot that I needed and ought to have the opportunities which cannot honestly be had without money, and I learned too late (as most learning by experience comes) that pecuniary anxieties disable a man in middle life more than ill health, or sorrow or overwork.[32]

IV *The Eternal City*

The old lawyer had one shot left in his locker, as his *Pilgrim* and *Alert* shipmates would have said. When his son married Edith Longfellow in 1878, Dana turned his practice over to him, moved to Europe, and hoped before the end of his life to write a stupendous book on international law. He also wanted to prepare an edition of his father's poetry, a history of the Dana family, and his own autobiography. Such works might have placed an ornamental crown upon his frequently pathetic life, if he could have carried them to completion. But fate intervened to delay his plans until death trampled them altogether.

Dana, his wife Sarah, and two of their daughters established their residence in Paris; and he worked about four hours daily at assembling his notes on international law.[33] At the same time he pardonably enjoyed a period of extended leisure in the captivating city, where he had spent a couple of frenzied days in 1856. In February, 1879, a cable informed him that his hearty old father was dead at last, at ninety-two. So Dana returned to America to settle the estate and also to tilt a final time with the redoubtable Lawrence. Perhaps uncandidly, Dana wrote his daughter that he was relishing the heady litigation.

If so, Europe interested him more now, for he was glad to return. Adams, who saw him just before his final farewell to his native land, describes him thus: "In his aspect there were none of the indications of anxiety, ill health or disappointment; on the contrary, he impressed me as being a strong, hale man of sixty, happy in his family and satisfied with his lot, enjoying the present and looking forward with satisfaction to the future."[34] Since his father had lived into his nineties, Dana might reasonably hope for a decade or even two of productive leisure.

After a second winter in Paris, he and Sarah spent the summer of 1880 in Versailles and then followed the fall to Geneva and Aix-les-Bains, where she wrote of him: "R. usually walked before breakfast, drinking the water—read & wrote mornings & walked after lunch & evenings."[35] Just before Christmas, 1880, they went to Rome; and Dana was enchanted by the matchless Eternal City. "One of the darling wishes of his heart [Adams writes] was now gratified, for he passed the winter at Rome and his daughter says she had rarely seen him so moved as by his first glimpse of the dome of St. Peter's across the Campagna."[36]

Dana, like other good Americans in Italy, became ever more ecstatic as he fell more and more in love with the magic land: "This is the land for you [he wrote home in 1881],—the land of beauty and romance,—the land of Naples, of Vesuvius, of burning craters and flowing lava, of vines, olives, figs, oranges, and lemons, of beauty in nature and art, in the human form and movement and voice, in the blue islands, the blue wave, and the violet hillsides. If you cross the Atlantic again, you must come here. It is a dream of life."[37]

And why not dream? Why hope that President James A. Garfield would see virtues in him which President Hayes had ignored? Why work on his literary projects? But Dana was uneasy in his old, still partially Calvinist conscience. After their glowing summer near Naples, he and Sarah went to Florence and then back to Rome in November. They had had an apartment at 104 Via Frattina, near the Spanish Steps; but soon they moved not far away to 86 Via Sistina.[38] All his notes were assembled at last. Before starting to write, Dana had meticulously read and critically annotated Hugo Grotius' *De Jure Belli et Pacis*, Théodore Funck-Bretano and Albert Sorel's *Précis du Droit des Gens*, Sir Edward Creasy's *First Platform of International Law*, Henry Wheaton's *History of the Law of Nations*, August Wilhelm Hefftner's *Völkerrecht den Gegenwart*, Joseph Louis Elzéar Ortolan's *Diplomatie de la Mer*, Sir Travers Twiss's *Law of Nations*, William Edward Hall's *International Law* (1880), and many other treatises, monographs, recent cases, and journal articles.[39]

105

Pathetically, within a couple of months after Dana started writing his treatise on international law, he became sick. Just before Christmas, 1881, he complained of chest pains; on Christmas Day he witnessed the inspiring if fatiguing ceremonies at St. Peter's; and then he dined most joyously with a group of fellow Americans at sculptor William Wetmore Story's apartment in Palazzo Barbarini. Three days after that he caught a severe chill in an open carriage ride around San Paolo fuori le Mura, past the Protestant Cemetery.[40]

Sarah's diary tells the story of the agonizing end. January 1, 1882: "My husband ill with pleuro-neumonia [sic] but progressing well. Dr. Aitken. I sit in his room now & write to my son. R. talks to himself all day incoherently but knows us." January 2: "R. had a bad night & the pain in chest was so violent that Dr. had to inject atropine, which quited [sic] the pain in a half hour but made him wild. He talked without cessation French & Italian & everything earthly, struggling to get out of bed constantly. . . ." January 3: "Today was comparatively comfortable until 5 P.M. when severe pain came . . ." January 4: "Wandering & wild all day, trying to get out of bed. talking incessantly not knowing us . . ."

January 5: "Dr. Aitken this morg. thought symptoms very bad. especially continued delirium & state of the kidneys (with albumen). He asked to have a consultation . . . Dr. Einhard—said it was a dangerous complication, but not imminent danger—We sent for Dr. Nevin & had prayers. . . ." January 6: "Richard dreadfully excited & full of spasmodic action in the night. After 5 or 7 quiet but in a comatose state wh. alarmed the Dr. . . . About 9½ after Dr. Nevin had seen my husband & prayed silently by him & just as he was preparing to read the 16 Psalm. Mr. Story came in, wh. fortunately kept him till the nurses came suddenly to the door & called: He went in, then returned & read the common prayer. And my husband was dead!"[41]

Richard Henry Dana, Jr., had probably wanted after death to join his many forebears in the Dana crypt at Cambridge, Massachusetts; but one fine spring day he and his wife had visited the Protestant Cemetery in Rome and were as moved by the beautiful place as Henry James had been a few years earlier. James pictured it this way:

Here is a mixture of tears and smiles, of stones and flowers, of mourning cypresses and radiant sky, which gives the impression of our looking back at death from the brighter side of the grave. The cemetery nestles in an angle of the city wall, and the older graves are sheltered by a mass of ancient brickwork, through whose narrow loopholes you peep at the wide purple of the Campagna. Shelley's grave is here, buried in roses . . . Nothing could be more impenetrably tranquil than this little corner in the bend of the protecting rampart, where a cluster of modern ashes is held tenderly in the rugged hand of the Past. The past is tremendously embodied in the hoary pyramid of Caius Cestius, which rises hard by, half within the wall and half without, cutting solidly into the solid blue of the sky and casting its pagan shadow upon the grass of English graves—that of Keats, among them—with an effect of poetic justice. It is a wonderful confusion of mortality and a grim enough admonition of our helpless promiscuity in the crucible of time. But the most touching element of all is the appeal of the pious inscriptions among all these Roman memories; touching because of their universal expression of that trouble within trouble, misfortune in a foreign land.[42]

When Sarah said of the lovely place during their visit there, "Is not this the spot where one would wish to lie forever?", Dana answered, "Yes, it is indeed!"[43] So, on January 8, 1882, his family buried him there.

107

CHAPTER 6

Two Years Before the Mast — Narrative, Structure and Form, Rhetoric

TWO YEARS BEFORE THE MAST is of primary value as a documentary, for most of what we know of Dana during his twenty-five months at sea and in California depends upon his own account. Without it, we could only sketchily reconstruct his 150 days from Boston to Santa Barbara, where he arrived on January 13, 1835; his varied experiences along the California coast from San Francisco to San Diego; and his epic 135-day voyage around Cape Horn in the worst possible weather and back home to Boston, where he docked on September 21, 1836. So, first of all, his book is a real-life narrative of actual experiences.

It may seem surprising that this fact should require emphasis, but, as Professor Lucid has pointed out, "As early as 1888 the unprejudiced . . . began confusing *Two Years* with fiction."[1] This forcing of *Two Years Before the Mast* into partly overlapping genres is really, however, a compliment to its vitality. In fact, it belongs in a small company including those few great American personal narratives whose movement, form, and symbolic values permit them to be considered as partly mythic. In various ways *Two Years Before the Mast* bears comparison with similar travel works by such American writers as Washington Irving, Herman Melville, Francis Parkman, Henry David Thoreau, Mark Twain, and in our century Ernest Hemingway. Dana's book, written earlier than most of the works of these men, also bears favorable comparison with many of theirs.

I Narrative

Two Years Before the Mast has a narrative movement as natural as day-night-day, summer-winter-summer, first year-second

year, and inexperience-experience. Dana takes us through a
sequence in real time, for real dates are periodically used in the
course of his narrative. In addition, he takes us on a real trip as
he records latitudes and longitudes to the minute. Since he uses
the same diary technique on the return trip, the book is assuredly
a loglike account; and it might have been more so but for the
fact that, when Dana returned to Boston, he entrusted his detailed sea diary to his cousin Frank Dana, and it unfortunately
disappeared. Dana therefore had only his excellent memory to
rely on, plus a ten-leaf notebook of matter-of-fact jottings.[2]

In addition to moving with Dana through time and space, we
watch him as he changes from a green hand to a self-reliant
seaman. We are no more bewildered than he when at the outset
he hears strange shouts which he should interpret as orders but
cannot. "Unintelligible orders were so rapidly given and so
immediately executed; there was such a scurrying about, and
such an intermingling of strange cries and stranger actions, that
I was completely bewildered. There is not so helpless and piti-
able an object in the world as a landsman beginning a sailor's
life (6).* This statement is straight credible fact, without the
fictional exaggeration which Melville and Twain, among others,
permit themselves in such initiation books as *Redburn, White-
Jacket, Roughing It,* and "Old Times on the Mississippi."

We sympathize when poor Dana is ordered aloft before he has
his sea legs. "How I got along, I cannot now remember. I 'laid out'
on the yards and held on with all my strength. I could not have
been of much service, for I remember having been sick several
times before I left the topsail yard" (10-11). Again the avoidance
of hyperbole is notable. The whole narrative is punctuated with
episodes proving that Dana is anxious to learn, to measure up to
the best of his shipmates. Once permitted to take his turn at the
helm, he does his trick well and thereafter insists upon doing
his share there too. Soon he may be seen jumping past more
experienced sailors to answer an order for difficult duty under
what most of us would call terrifying conditions. When his betters
perform the intricate duty of sending down a royal-yard, he
watches for the one purpose of doing it well himself:

---

* All parenthetical references in this chapter and the next are to Dana,
Two Years Before the Mast (Los Angeles, 1964).

> . . . an old sailor, whose favor I had taken some pains to gain, had taught me carefully everything which was necessary to be done, and in its proper order . . . I told the second mate . . . that I could do it, and got him to ask the mate to send me up the first time they [the royal-yards] were struck. Accordingly I was called upon, and went up, repeating the operations over in my mind, taking care to get everything in its order, for the slightest mistake spoils the whole. Fortunately, I got through without any word from the officer, and heard the "well done" of the mate, when the yard reached the deck, with as much satisfaction as I ever felt at Cambridge on seeing a *"bene"* at the foot of a Latin exercise. (77)

In becoming adept, Dana had to overcome the disadvantage of being known as a well-born Bostonian and a college man. When he first saw Hawaiians carrying hides on their heads to load them into a boat, his look of dismay was probably responsible for a sly crack at his background. " 'Well, D[ana],' said the second mate to me, 'this does not look much like Cambridge college, does it? This is what I call *"head work"* ' " (64). Given his first shore leave, at San Diego, Dana apparently preferred horses to liquor but wanted to avoid seeming to snub his thirsty cronies. So he and Stimson had to go with them to the first grogshop, where they stood one another drinks, the oldest buying first according to protocol, before they could slip out and rent a pair of horses.

Dana remained an admirable combination of friendly mate and self-assertive blueblood. During the smoking of the *Alert,* the crew sealed the forecastle without thinking to bring out any reading material. Then one man remembered that he had left a copy of Sir Walter Scott's *Woodstock* in the galley:

> This was a great windfall, and as all could not read it at once, I, being the scholar of the company, was appointed reader. I got a knot of six or eight about me, and no one could have had a more attentive audience. Some laughed at the "scholars," and went over the other side of the forecastle, to work, and spin their yarns: but I carried the day, and had the cream of the crew for my hearers. Many of the reflections, and the political parts, I omitted, but all the narrative they were delighted with . . . Many things which, while I

was reading, I had a misgiving about, thinking them above
their capacity, I was surprised to find them enter into completely. (254)

His most grievous brush with the *hoi polloi* occurred when
Captain Thompson agreed to let him ship home aboard the
Alert but ordered English Ben to leave her and report to the
Pilgrim in Dana's place. " 'Oh yes!' said the crew, 'the captain
has let you off, because you are a gentleman's son, and have got
friends, and know the owners; and taken Ben, because he is
poor, and has got nobody to say a word for him!' " (262). Dana
went to Ben's rescue but only by buying a different replacement
for half a year's wages.

At the same time Dana is narrating his story he is also giving
us a book of facts. He knows that his readers are likely to be
landlubbers; so he realistically tells us about sails, spars, rigging,
bells, watches, life forward and life aft, living in the steerage
and moving to the forecastle, anchoring, slipping cables, beating
to windward, heaving-to, eating from the kid, sleeping, washing,
mending clothes, and making hats.

When the sailors go ashore, the same pattern appears again.
Dana looks all about him with the careful eye of Parkman at
Fort Laramie or Thoreau at Walden, and records all that he
sees. And even while he is telling us what he did, loading hides,
running messages, gathering wood, he also informs us about the
geography of Monterey, Italian boat-songs, the diet of Russian
sailors, San Diego horses, the garb of Mexican customs officers,
a funeral parade to the Mission of Santa Barbara, the natural
goodness of Hawaiian sailors, and much else. These gratuitous
details may occasionally be more than we care to read through,
but there is an aptness in the reader's being initiated into the
mysteries of life before the mast and in California in the 1830's
by Dana, who was a novice too at the outset of his adventures.

II *Structure and Form*

Whether he knew it or not, Dana worked his material into a
balanced shape which is, in part, independent of his story. Like
almost any account of a trip away from home to a strange place
and then back again, *Two Years Before the Mast* has a sonata

111

form. On his way to California, Dana is tested as to his obedi-
ence, adroitness, strength, alertness, and powers of observation.
In California, he is tested anew, under different circumstances,
and in a partly different setting. On his way back home, the first
tests are repeated, but then comes the final challenge: Cape
Horn in mid-winter. This three-part structure is somewhat similar
to the exposition, development, and recapitulation of the sonata.
For good measure, Dana later added a coda in the form of a
"Concluding Chapter," later replacing it by his afterword,
"Twenty-Four Years Later," which is the romantic story of his
nostalgic return to California in 1859.

Two Years Before the Mast has thirty-six chapters. The first
eight (I-VIII) tell of the voyage to California. The next twenty
chapters (IX-XXVIII) describe Dana's California duties and
pleasures. The last eight chapters (XXIX-XXXVI) tell of ready-
ing the ship and then voyaging home to Boston. Thus we have
a tidy 8-20-8-chapter structure.

Several events in early chapters are echoed in precisely cor-
responding late chapters. For example, in Chapter I the *Pilgrim*
leaves Boston, and in Chapter XXXVI the *Alert* returns to Boston. In Chapter II Dana is violently seasick; in Chapter XXXV he
is virtually the only man aboard who is not seasick. Chapters IV
and XXXIII feature arguments between Captain Thompson and
his officers. In Chapters V and XXXII Dana doubles the Cape.
In Chapter VI George Ballmer falls overboard and is lost; in
Chapter XXXI Dana is forced below by a violent toothache
which endangers his life. And, as we have seen, in Chapter VIII
the *Pilgrim* reaches California, while in Chapter XXIX the *Alert*
leaves California.

The same sort of unconscious echoing may be noted but to a
lesser extent in the twenty-chapter middle section of the narrative. Thus, in Chapter X the *Pilgrim* picks up its first passengers
bound for Monterey, and in Chapter XXVI some Mexican passengers board the *Alert* at Monterey. And in Chapter XVI Dana
reluctantly follows his mates into the grogshop; in Chapter XXI
he uncandidly tells us that he never saw a drunken Mexican.[3]
Obviously, some of these arching echoes are merely coincidental;
but, taken together and with the 8-20-8-chapter breakdown, they
give Dana's book something of the shape of a Gothic façade.

Other principles of balance operate through the book. Exactly halfway through it in terms of pages, Dana describes an event of central importance which occurred when he was exactly halfway in time through his twenty-five-month Odyssey. On August 30, 1835, Dana boarded the *Alert* in the harbor of San Diego and talked with the members of her crew who had not gone ashore to take advantage of their first Sunday liberty there. This visit led to his applying to Captain Thompson for permission to transfer to that ship, which was granted and accomplished in a week. Thus the first half of the book concerns Dana and the *Pilgrim;* the second, Dana and the *Alert.*

Furthermore, fate divided Dana's California duties into temporal units of roughly equal lengths which are approximately echoed in the structure of his accounts of them. For his first four months in California—from January 14 to May 8, 1835—he was a busy crew member of a vessel plying up and down the coast. Dana then cured hides ashore for the next four months—May 8 to September 8. Halfway through this period Dana was finished with his first consignment of hides and therefore was able to rest. Then on July 8 the *Pilgrim* reappeared and brought him more hides, and with them a renewal of work. September 8 was his first day of duty aboard the *Alert;* and eight months later to the day she left San Diego for Boston, carrying Dana with her, to his infinite relief. Curiously, Dana bid farewell to San Diego on May 8, one year to the day after he first began hide-curing there.

Unfortunately, Dana does not have a unit of six chapters cover, say, a four-month unit of time. Therefore the symmetry provided by the 8-20-8-chapter structure does not in any sense harmonize with the temporal progression just summarized. In fact, when Dana is at the midpoint in terms of chapters, that is, when he is ending Chapter XVIII, he has arrived only at May 8, 1835, and therefore has accounted for only about one third of his twenty-five months. It may be concluded, therefore, that Dana's blocks of pages more accurately reflect the steady flow of time over the months than do his blocks of chapters which concern events. It is also noteworthy that the first twelve chapters are less than two-thirds the length of the second twelve chapters and less than one-half the length of the last twelve chapters. Moreover, in the first third, chapters are erratically different in length; in the second third, the limits are much closer together; they are also in the last third, which, however, shows a slightly wider spread. These time-chapter discrepancies probably mean simply that when Dana began to write he was unsure of himself and hence broke his composition into irregular, choppy chapters; then, by the time he had gained confidence and was well into narrating his California experiences, he planned and wrote more steadily; finally, the last chapters perhaps betray a little haste in adding recollections previously omitted and also in getting on home to Boston, once the Cape has been successfully doubled.

Far more important than any mathematical demonstrations is an awareness that the experiences which *Two Years Before the Mast* unfolds were living ones—and through Dana's art are living still. We accept Dana's credentials; his narrative has the ring of authenticity; and we believe his story. But this effect is not enough to guarantee living art. Chance divided his experiences into three parts in such a way that his account is esthetically pleasing through having the beginning, middle, and end prescribed by Aristotle.[4] But the book still would not have come to life if Dana had not brilliantly employed two techniques— telling the truth exactly as he saw and felt it, and shifting certain episodes out of chronological order to brighten otherwise dull sections.

At first it may seem a waste of time to read that Dana aimed to give a truthful picture of life at sea. But, as Professor Thomas Philbrick has demonstrated, American writers before Dana generally sentimentalized the sailor and romanticized his wild enemy the sea. By the 1830's a timid new note of realism began to be heard, and the public and the critics alike were pleased.[5] Then came Dana. In his original preface, dated July, 1840, he explains his purpose very clearly indeed:

> In the following pages I design to give an accurate and authentic narrative of a little more than two years spent as a common sailor, before the mast, in the American merchant service. . . . I have adhered closely to fact in every particular, and endeavored to give each thing its true character. In so doing, I have been obliged occasionally to use strong and coarse expressions, and in some instances to give scenes which may be painful to nice feelings; but I have very carefully avoided doing so, whenever I have not felt them essential to giving the true character of a scene. My design is, and it is this which has induced me to publish the book,

to present the life of a common sailor at sea as it really is,—
the light and the dark together. (xxi-xxii)

Thus Dana's practice anticipated by many years William Dean
Howells' theory that Realism is nothing more nor less than the
truthful treatment of material. And Dana's statement—if not
always his accomplishment—more dramatically predates, by almost a century, Ernest Hemingway's celebrated application of
Gertrude Stein's theories. Early in *Death in the Afternoon,* Hemingway explains his purpose as follows: ". . . I found the greatest
difficulty, aside from knowing what you truly felt, rather than
what you were supposed to feel, and had been taught to feel,
was to put down what really happened in action; what the actual
things were which produced the emotion that you experienced."[6]
Like Hemingway, Dana must have found it difficult to know what
he really felt rather than what he was supposed romantically to
feel. Also he must often have surprised himself by writing more
realistic descriptions of "the actual things . . . which produced
the emotion" than he could find precedent for in his somewhat
limited reading. It is remarkable that, given his past, he was able
to be as frank and honest as he was with himself and his readers.

All the more noteworthy is Dana's achievement when we consider that his technique of accurate reporting appears to work
at cross purposes with another technique that he adopted—that
of occasionally shifting incidents out of chronological order. Dana
tries to "give each thing its true character" as he tells his story
faithfully, but at the same time he often reorders for variety and
emphasis. His preface implies that he was more conscious of his
use of the first technique than of the second. It took skill in the
use of both, however, for Dana to give his book its well-paced
verisimilitude.

One example should suffice to show that Dana can give us the
sense of being there with him.

September 22d . . . upon coming on deck at seven bells in
the morning, we found the other watch aloft throwing water
upon the sails; and looking astern, we saw a small clipper-
built brig with a black hull heading directly after us. We
went to work immediately, and put all the canvass upon the
brig which we could get upon her, rigging out oars for stud-
ding-sail yards; and continued wetting down the sails by

buckets of water whipped up to the mast-head, until about nine o'clock, when there came on a drizzling rain. The vessel continued in pursuit, changing her course as we changed ours, to keep before the wind. The captain, who watched her with his glass, said that she was armed, and full of men, and showed no colors. We continued running dead before the wind, knowing that we sailed better so, and that clippers are fastest *on* the wind. We had also another advantage. The wind was light, and we spread more canvass than she did, having royals and sky-sails fore and aft, and ten studding-sails; while she, being an hermaphrodite brig, had only a gaff topsail, aft. (22)

Notice that, like Dana, we are oblivious of the danger until we get on deck with him. With him we observe something unusual: the watch we are to relieve is still at work, remarkably throwing water on the sails to increase the speed of the ship. We wonder why and only then look astern to see the danger. It is a brig, clipper-built and black-hulled. It is uncannily apt that Dana gives us only these details at this time—type of build and then color of hull. There is no time for more observation. "We went to work immediately . . ." More sails must be put on, and at once. The fact that oars are rigged for extra yards is suggestive: there is not time to get out stowed spare spars. After all available canvas is spread, all hands whip up buckets of water to the very masthead. When it starts to rain, this operation is no longer necessary, and the crew can pause and only then note the time. An hour and a half has passed, and the enemy brig is still in pursuit. We change course, and so does she. Only now can time be spared to hear the captain's report: she is armed, full of men, and without colors. The situation is highly unusual, or Captain Thompson would not bother to inform his crew. We run dead before the wind, to reduce the advantage of the pursuing clipper, which sails fastest on the wind. Now that we can take the time to think about her position and also examine in more detail the nature of the enemy, we note another advantage which the light wind gives us: the pursuing vessel is a hermaphrodite brig, and hence is schooner-rigged aft.

The entire report is masterly, giving us impressions and thoughts, and in the same order in which they came to Dana. In this passage—and dozens like it—we see and hear with him; and the emphasis is on sensation, with a minimum of time out for thought. He does indeed "present the life of a common sailor at sea as it really is . . ."

Two Years Before the Mast is not merely a log or sea-diary, taking up a sequence of stirring and dull sensations and circumstances in the order of their occurrence. Professor Hart goes so far as to suggest that it was perhaps fortunate that Dana's notebook was lost, that his consequent reliance upon his romantic memory resulted in his preserving the proper "distance" from his material.[7] In any event, variety if not distance was one of his conscious aims.

Let us now consider an example of the shifting of events out of chronological order for the purpose of achieving variety. After Dana has starkly reported in Chapter VI the death by drowning of George Ballmer, he closes the chapter by turning to the Negro cook. Dana writes: "The night after this event [Ballmer's death], when I went to the galley to light my cigar, I found the cook inclined to be talkative, so I sat down on the spars, and gave him an opportunity to hold a yarn. I was the more inclined to do so, as I found that he was full of superstitions once more common among seamen, and which the recent death had waked up in his mind" (39). What follows is an amusing record, partly in inconsistent dialect, of the cook's attitude toward dreams, the shadow cast ahead by death approaching, the legend of the Flying Dutchman, and the wizardry of Finns. This gay close to an otherwise solemn chapter reminds us all that we should not look too steadily at death, that life does go absurdly on. The belief that Dana tacked this ending to Chapter VI for relief gains support by the fact that in his little ten-page journal he penciled this entry beside the date May 8, 1835: "superstit. Cook. sailmaker."[8] It will be recalled that Ballmer had drowned six months earlier.

Other examples may be found in Chapter XXXV, the next to last. It opens with what is almost a confession that the chronological approach is tedious, especially now that the voyage is nearly over.

> From the latitude of the West Indies, until we got inside the Bermudas, . . . we had every variety of weather, and two or three moderate gales, . . . of which one is a specimen of all.
> —A fine afternoon; all hands at work, some in the rigging,

and others on deck; a stiff breeze, and ship close upon the wind, and sky-sails brailed down.—Latter part of the afternoon, breeze increases . . . Spray begins to fly . . . One of the boys furls the mizen royal.—Cook thinks there is going to be 'nasty work,' and has supper ready early. . . . While eating supper, hear the watch on deck taking in the royals.—Coming on deck, find it is blowing harder, and an ugly head sea running. . . . Clouds look black and wild; wind rising, and . . . (330)

This is less a shifting of events than it is a compressing of many into one. But later in the same chapter, taking potatoes and onions from a passing brig back to the *Alert* reminds Dana of a humorous story a sailor on the *Pilgrim* used to tell. Dana is anxious not to forget it any longer, and also perhaps feels that telling it now will reinforce the sense that the *Alert* is happy to be coming close to home. Then, in order to set the stage properly for the climactic battle between the mate Brown and the steward on the *Alert*, Dana says that "They had been on bad terms the whole voyage; and had threatened a rupture several times" (322). Thus it seems that Dana delayed telling of this antagonism until the end of Chapter XXXIII, which, being mainly about smooth sailing six weeks from home, needed spicing. In fact, the manner in which Dana avoids the strictly chronological order all through Chapters XXXIII, XXXIV, and XXXV is highly commendable.

In the California narrative Dana also paces what might have been a merely reportorial account. Professor Lucid's study of the small notebook shows that Dana shifts the time he chooses to report the funeral of the little girl in San Pedro and also his attendance at the cockfight (both Chapter XVIII) "to distribute interesting and colorful anecdotes more effectively."[9] Chapter XXI is entirely informational: it briefly (and inaccurately[10]) sketches the historical background of California; tells of its social, political, and religious confusion; introduces a criminal incident which Dana evidently saw; and ends with an implicit prophecy as to California's future greatness. Appearing as it does in the midst of the hide-house section (Chapters XIX-XXII), Chapter XXI is a welcome interlude in an account of what in real life was probably arduous tedium. Other examples are numerous

118

of the shifting of material out of chronological or otherwise normal order.

Thus, all mature readers must conclude that Dana used real skill in evoking the sensations he had before the mast and in California, and we must also praise him for so pacing his narrative as to keep us from boredom even while he includes boredom as one of the many sensations he reports. The result is enduring organic art, a story "so passionate and alive that like the spirit of a plant or an animal it has an architecture of its own"—to take up Emerson's famous words from his essay "The Poet."[11]

Dana was fortunate. His adventures were cyclical and yet progressive, and hence his book has the contours of the great patterns of nature. His details are natural and functional. He puts them forth not to embellish or to boast, but because they all help to clarify his subject—the plight of the sailor at sea and ashore. Schematically as well as rhetorically, *Two Years Before the Mast* is often rough and imperfect. But one may call it organic because it is vibrant, has approximate symmetry, and contains functionally related parts.

III Rhetoric

Two Years Before the Mast is one of the most immediately appealing and constantly absorbing books in American literature. As John T. Winterich, who has assessed its popularity, correctly says, "Dana had the rare gift of simple, straight-forward, lucid utterance. He is one of the few writers who are completely understandable. . . . Is it any wonder that even today [1955] extracts from *Two Years Before the Mast* are used by ophthalmologists and optometrists? Go to your eyeman and take a test—you will be reading a universal English that neither dismays the dullard nor patronizes the intellectual."[12]

Such praise is typical, but it may tend to obscure the fact that parts of *Two Years Before the Mast* are badly written. When critics were still little boys and girls, they read it as they read *Huckleberry Finn;* grown up, they too often ignore it as a juvenile untouchable. But it seems high time to list and briefly consider its compositional deficiencies. It is marred to some extent by grammatical errors, careless mechanics, imperfect editing, and timidity. Like Charles Dickens, whom Dana later reluctantly stooped to meet, he wrote badly enough to ruin his work and yet vibrantly enough for it to survive. Like many another awkward genius—for example, Victor Hugo and James Fenimore Cooper—Dana can be most thrilling when he is rhetorically least admirable. The entire thirty-first chapter, for one instance, is shot through with awkwardnesses and yet is probably the most exciting chapter in the entire book.

Dana's most dramatic type of grammatical error is the dangling modifier, of which there are almost thirty in the book, most of them in the second half. We find four in Chapter XXXIII alone, beginning with this one: "Waiting for a good opportunity, the halyards were manned . . ." (316). Usually the danglers are simple present participles, but some are hilarious past participles: "Having washed down decks and got our breakfast, the two vessels lay side by side . . ." (267). A few are less reprehensibly gerundive: ". . . in coming home from round Cape Horn, . . . the north star is the first land you make" (280). But the gem of all Dana's verbal danglers is the following, from late in the final chapter: "At one tack we ran so near to Rainsford Island, that, looking down from the royal yard, the island . . . seemed to lie directly under our yard-arm" (342).

Dana also composes dangling prepositional phrases ("In this state [Dana has a toothache], the steward applied to the captain for some rice to boil for me" [291]); infinitives ("Indeed, to show the entire want of any sense of morality or domestic duty among them, I have frequently known an Indian to bring his wife . . . down to the beach, and carry her back again, dividing with her the money which she had got from the sailors" [171]); elliptical clauses ("While on deck, the regular work of the ship went on" [181]); and even one squinting dangling gerundive phrase—"The next day being Sunday, after washing and clearing decks, and getting breakfast, the mate came forward with leave for one watch to go ashore, on liberty. We drew lots . . ." (117).[13]

Minor grammatical errors committed by Dana are of six or eight different sorts. He confuses adjectives and adverbs, as in "We sailed leisurely" (111) and "An old sailor . . . said he felt disagreeably" (336). He places "only" too early, as in informal writing, unlike his own, and as in present-day speech; thus, "that routine of sea-life which is only broken by a storm" (13) and

"The watches were only varied by taking the helm in turn" (218). Dana uses "and which" and like constructions after omitting the first "which": "a thing hardly ever heard of, and which the sailors had ridiculed" (316); and "Some persons we see under no remarkable circumstances, but whom . . . we never forget" (91). Parallelism is occasionally violated, as when "Nicholas . . . neither knew how to read or write" (155). Finally, Dana could so far forget his rules of grammar as to write as follows: ". . . there is snow and rain, gales and high seas, in abundance" (274); "No person could have told, from the heavens, by their eyesight alone, that it was not a still summer's night" (214); and "Twenty-three guns followed in regular succession, with an interval of fifteen seconds between each" (236).

Related to Dana's imperfect grammar is his careless punctuation. Admittedly times and practices have changed, but should we forgive the following strange usages? ". . . [W]e finished curing all our hides . . . and got in readiness for the arrival of the ship, and had another spell of three or four weeks; which I spent, as usual, in reading, writing, studying, making and mending my clothes, and getting my wardrobe in complete readiness, in case I should go on board the ship; and in fishing, ranging the woods with the dogs, and in occasional visits to the presidio and mission" (174). And "Toward night a moderate breeze sprang up; the fog however continuing as thick as before; and we kept on to the eastward" (340).

Dana affects the logical double or nearly double negative, slightly inappropriate literary allusions, and capricious quotation marks. Evenly spaced through the book are more than a score of usually pretentious double negatives, three of them in one paragraph: "not a little frightened," "not excepting Old Bill and the cook," and "We . . . chuckled not a little" (284). Occasionally the usage results in an unnautical indirectness: ". . . but the shark at last got off [away from two Hawaiians], carrying away a hook and line, and not a few severe bruises" (166). On one occasion the construction is combined with unintended ambiguity: ". . . we commenced getting under weigh, and were not a little while about it" (45).[14]

Various experiences often trigger literary associations in Dana, whether they are apt or not. Thus, when he thinks of the wretched weather to which sailors are exposed (19), *King Lear*

(III, i) comes to mind, in which the gentleman describes the frightful storm buffeting the king. Later, roping himself down the dizzy cliff of San Juan to dislodge hides, Dana again supposedly thinks (142) of *King Lear*—this time of Edgar's thrilling description of the samphire-gatherers' view (IV, vi). The thought that he and his shipmates may well die in the ice fields off Cape Horn reminds Dana (304) of Claudio's famous soliloquy on death in *Measure for Measure* (III, i). Dana is skillful at weaving quotations into his text, and yet they certainly make him more bookish than he actually was at the time.

In addition to English quotations, Dana loads his text with a good deal of unnautical Latin lumber. Curiously, such Latin tags as "auctoritate mihi commissâ" (250) and "ipso facto" (322) appear when Dana is discussing the separation of one person—often himself—from others. Twice Latin is cleverly used. While sitting on a hide in San Diego trimming fat off it, Dana was approached and addressed by Captain Faucon, former commander of the *Alert*, who said, "Tityre, tu patulae recubans sub tegmine fagi"—"Tityrus, you lie under the cover of the spreading beech-tree." Dana continued, "Very apropos, thought I, and, at the same time, serves to show that you have studied Latin" (165). Perhaps the line has ironic appropriateness, since Dana is anything but a Tityrus resting in the shade of a *fagus;* possibly Faucon expected Dana to continue the quotation with "nos patriam fugimus," which appears three lines later in Virgil's *First Eclogue.* Then, as Dana contemplated bidding the cliffs of San Juan farewell at last, the stoic lines of Aeneas occurred to him: " 'Forsitan et haec olim [meminisse iuvabit],' thought I . . ." (252)—"Perhaps someday it will be a pleasure to remember even this." The line is apt, for, as he recites it in the *Aeneid* (I, 203), Aeneas is standing on a coastal peak in Libya, with his past far behind and his destiny obscure.

Other literary references make even clearer the romantic streak in Dana. He approached the Island of Juan Fernandez agog because of having read *Robinson Crusoe* as a child. He pressed a flower from the island between pages of Cowper's *Letters.* And he ravenously fell on such reading fare as Edward Bulwer-Lytton's *Paul Clifford,* William Godwin's *Mandeville,* and Sir Walter Scott's *Pirate* and *Woodstock.*

If esoteric literary references tend to separate Dana from his cohorts before the mast, his manner of using quotation marks shows his distance even more. Surely it would have been better if he had more naturally incorporated nautical jargon and slang into his text, or had explained them from the side of the sailors, so to speak. This is the method of Melville in *Typee, White-Jacket,* and *Moby Dick,* and of Twain in *Roughing It* and "Old Times on the Mississippi." But, instead, Dana's quotation marks imply both his initial landlubberliness and his occasional sense of aloof superiority. When, for example, Dana and his shipmates come off duty wet and cold, they are allowed a pot of tea, "or [Dana adds], as the sailors significantly call it, 'water bewitched' " (33). We are told that "if you live in the forecastle, you are 'as independent as a wood-sawyer's clerk,' (nauticé), and are a *sailor*" (52). Often a nautical expression is graphic, as when a raging gale is said to be " 'blowing like scissors and thumbscrews' " (216). Dana sometimes credits sailors with clichés: " 'The more, the merrier' is the sailor's maxim" (187). Carefully encased in quotation marks are nautical expressions which were fresh to Dana's ear—and to the eyes of his readers—but which are platitudinous today, for example, "knock off," "know the ropes," ship-shape," and "three sheets to the wind."[15]

Inevitably, an author like Dana, part of whose purpose is to familiarize the reader with processes strange to him, at times puts into quotation marks and even laboriously defines what is obvious, while elsewhere he will not explain at all what is truly esoteric. Thus, Dana describes a rustic group of seamen as follows: "His boat's crew were a pretty raw set, just out of the bush, and, as the sailor's phrase is, 'hadn't got the hayseed out of their hair' " (34-35). The cliché is repeated later: ". . . the greater part of the crew were raw hands, just from the bush, as green as cabbages, and had not yet got the hay-seed [not hayseed] out of their heads" (209). Yet Dana pictures a slovenly whaling ship as having "clumsy seizing and straps without covers, and homeward-bound splices" (209), and he can as enigmatically complain later that "The prospect of another year after the *Alert* should sail, was rather 'too much of the monkey' " (187). Worse, he can load page after page with seaman's jargon, to the utter dismay of the average reader. Thus, John the French sailor secures the main royal by "frapping it with long pieces of sinnet" (215); in milder weather "As the brig came more upon the wind, she felt it more, and we doused the sky-sails, but kept the weather studding-sails on her, bracing the yards forward so that the swinging-boom nearly touched the sprit-sail yard" (73). Bewildering sequences of nautical talk appear throughout the whole book. It must be added, however, that even when one cannot fully comprehend the lingo used, the effect is often thrilling.

Dana perhaps consciously employs this method of presentation to keep his readers alert. Certainly we learn much about life at sea—about booms, brailings, earings, gaffs, geswarps, hawsers, martingales, robands, scuttled butt, slush, tholepins, and the like. *Two Years Before the Mast* is also a treasury of such recondite nautical expressions as *duff, fake, grub, holidays, Irish pendants,* and *scouse*—among other terms. Sometimes Dana confidentially uses them with no definition; sometimes he explains parenthetically or in footnotes.

A final point might be usefully made concerning mechanics of composition. Dana too often uses an odd word without explanation, and then only later defines it. Three examples are *soger* (used on pp. 23 and 79, footnoted on p. 128), *kid* (used on pp. 33 and 34, defined on p. 179), and *holystone* (used on pp. 164, 176, and 178, defined on p. 179). Related to this amateurish habit is his occasional practice of twice explaining the same expression or practice, for example *rattled up* (pp. 49 and 335) and the necessity of making a joke of serious matters at sea (pp. 34, 247, and 324). Once in a while, Dana repeats his identification of a person; for example, the *Alert* third mate Mr. Hatch is named and identified twice (pp. 259 and 312), and yet earlier (pp. 178 and 187) his activities are described without his being named at all.[16]

Two Years Before the Mast may be imperfectly written from a rhetorician's point of view. But it is an exciting, informative narrative all the same, well constructed to show its author's mutations. In addition, its tonal and mythic qualities, and the ways in which it may be compared with other American journey books, make it perennially appealing to all kinds of readers.

CHAPTER 7

Two Years Before the Mast — Tone, Myth, Journey

I *Tone*

In *Two Years Before the Mast* Dana maintains a consistent attitude toward his material. Like Ernest Hemingway, he sees himself as facing an adventurous challenge. He regards the sea and the primitive land as simply two environments in which he can meet his tests, rather than the embodiment of primodial, malignant forces. Although Dana takes himself with Brahministic seriousness, he regards his cohorts as proper subjects for occasional humor. He repeatedly says that a sailor must make and take jokes, but he almost never shows himself being made a fool of, as for example Melville and Twain often do.

Dana set out to present "the light and dark together." He succeeded, and therefore *Two Years Before the Mast* is often quite funny. The first humor, however, comes only after Dana has got his sea legs, has begun to prove himself a man, and then sees Juan Fernandez. Laughed at by the seasoned crew for his haste in volunteering to go ashore, Dana in turn looks down upon the island natives, who "seemed to me to be the laziest people on the face of the earth. They did nothing but take a *paseo* into the woods, a *paseo* among the houses, a *paseo* at the landing-place, looking at us and our vessel, and too lazy to speak fast . . ." (44).

Too quick to ridicule all natives, Dana adopts the same essentially provincial attitude toward Mexicans and Indians on the coast, calling "The Californians . . . an idle, thriftless people" (82). He is annoyed once when some Indians merely stand around uncooperatively while their American visitors sweat away carrying cargo "California fashion" up a hill which oxen cannot climb; he pictures the onlookers as "the lazy Indians, who came down with them [the carts], squatting down on their hams, looking on, doing nothing, and when we asked them to help us, only shaking their heads, or drawling out 'no quiero' " (100).

Later, when Dana notes that the Mexicans merely shake their heads and mutter "Caramba" at the drenching the sailors get in the surf as they launch their boats, he is irrationally offended again: "They had no taste for such doings; in fact, the hydrophobia is a national malady, and shows itself in their persons as well as their actions" (211). Probably not intended to be humorous, but having an almost Twain-like effect on the reader all the same, is Dana's description of a sick old Mexican spotted near the Mission of San Diego: "He had a few grey hairs, which were tied together at the back of his head; and he was so feeble that, when we came up to him, he raised his hands slowly to his face, and taking hold of his lids with his fingers, lifted them up to look at us; and being satisfied, let them drop again" (122).

Dana's humor gains its effects by focusing on ludicrous incidents, flirts timidly with sexual matters once in a while, is reinforced by mordant understatement and abandoned overstatement, often uses simple irony, and three times breaks into darkly bitter sarcasm. Dana so rarely exhibits wit that, if the reader suspects its presence, he is safer to suspect himself.

In two long years, incidents would inevitably develop to provoke laughter. Thus, when Captain Thompson sees that his *Pilgrim* is certain to crash into the the *Loriotte* in San Diego Harbor, he sits down on the rail and yells out to the captain of the endangered vessel nearby that he is coming to visit. When the men are ordered to take the cook's pet pig ashore, they put her in a sling and then hoist her all the way up to the yardarm. And upon noticing that Mr. Bingham, a Hawaiian resident of the abandoned oven, has had two front teeth knocked out as evidence of grief over the death of Kamehameha I, the Yankees accuse him of having lost his teeth by eating Captain Cook. Each incident is a raucous little interlude quickly ended, and none takes much time to tell.

Given the period in which he wrote, Dana was obliged to play down sexual elements. For example, when he and his friends go aboard the *Lagoda* in San Diego Harbor for the usual bull session with her crew, all we are treated to by way of report is the following: "Then followed conversation which one must always hear in a ship's forecastle, and which, bad as it is, is no worse, nor, indeed, more gross, than that of many well-dressed young gentlemen at their clubs" (115). Nor are we given anything but the mildest and least offensive lines from one of the most anemic love songs of the English man-of-war's men who visit the hide-house. Dana's account of the Indian who transported his wife down to the Yankee beachhead near the hide-house and back again later, "dividing with her the money which she had got from the sailors" (171), is only sententiously critical.[1]

When Dana insisted upon improving his free time on the beach by studying Spanish, he must have suffered a good deal of ribbing, which he chooses not to record. He does tell us that the coarse crew jibed heartlessly at "Chips," the newly married carpenter whose wife did not write him for six months; but Dana does not repeat any of the jokes. Expunged by Dana from the manuscript of *Two Years Before the Mast* before it went to the printer was a uniquely frank comment on the strangeness of the Hawaiian Hope's contracting venereal disease at San Diego "when he did seem to have not so many women & them not so much from inclination but as from its being almost a part of daily life; yet he was the first to suffer & the one to suffer most."[2]

Dana employs humorous litotes and hyperbole with as much control as Melville and Twain but less often. Thus, in foul weather "All hands were called to 'come up and see it rain'" (97); caught out overnight in a skiff, the wood-gathering detail finds "knotty logs rather indifferent couches" (224); and to celebrate Christmas, the grease-eating Russian sailors in Monterey "had a grand blow-out, and (as our men said) drank, in the forecastle, a barrel of gin, ate up a [hide] bag of tallow, and made a soup of the skin" (226).

Occasionally nautical dialogue is humorously used, best perhaps when one old tar ventures an explanation of Professor Nuttall, the Harvard naturalist who collects specimens in California:

"Oh, 'vast there!—You don't know anything about them craft. I've seen them colleges, and know the ropes. They keep all such things for cur'osities, and study 'em, and have men a' purpose to go and get 'em. This old chap knows what he's about. He a'n't the fool you take him for. He'll carry all these

things to the college, and if they are better than any that
they have had before, he'll be head of the college. Then,
by-and-by, somebody else will go after some more, and if
they beat him, he'll have to go again, or else give up his
berth. That's the way they did make the spun yarn. This
old covey knows the ropes. He has worked a traverse over
'em, and come 'way out here, where nobody's even been
afore, and where they'll never think of coming." (277-78)

But Dana steps back to his distance from his subject when he
concludes the passage as follows: "This explanation satisfied
Jack . . ." (278).

Dana should have seen fit to unbend and report more such
graphic talk as the colorful comment by an officer to the hand
who mistook vast chunks of ice for land: "'Land in your eye!'
said the mate, who was looking through the telescope; 'they are
ice islands, if I can see a hole through a ladder!'" (305). Dana
apparently did not wish to get down to the level of the ordinary
seaman and stay there for any length of time. In fact, a speech
by one character is reported partly in dialect and partly not:
"'I'm plaguy glad o' dat,' said the cook. 'I was mighty 'fraid he
was a Fin. I tell you what, I been plaguy civil to that man all the
voyage'" (40).

With only three exceptions, Dana's irony is simple almost to
the point of puerility. Tediously he writes of pleasure and satisfaction when he means displeasure and dissatisfaction, as in "the
pleasant prospect of beating up to Monterey . . . against a violent
head wind" (74) and "the satisfaction of seeing [from the rig-
ging] the Italian ship's boat go ashore, filled with men [on
leave]" (137). Once his tone is so neutral that the irony may be
only imaginary; "No sooner was the importance of the country
[of California] known, than the Jesuits obtained leave to establish themselves in it, to christianize and enlighten the Indians"
(167). Dana was a conservative Christian; so the word "enlighten" is probably used without any intended irony.

Three times Dana is bleakly—and most effectively—ironic.
First, he and his mates are worked so frequently on Sundays that
they envy the *Rosa*'s Catholic crew:

> The Easter holydays are kept up on shore during three days;
> and being a Catholic vessel, the crew had the advantage of
> them. For two successive days, while perched up on the

rigging, covered with tar and engaged in our disagreeable work, we saw these fellows going ashore in the morning, and coming off again at night, in high spirits. So much for being Protestants. There's no danger of Catholicism's spreading in New England; Yankees can't afford the time to be Catholics. American ship-masters get nearly three weeks more labor out of their crews, in the course of a year, than the masters of vessels from Catholic countries. Yankees don't keep Christmas, and ship-masters at sea never know when Thanksgiving comes, so Jack has no festival at all. (137)

Next, rounding Cape Horn, Dana and his mates are numb with cold and quaking with fatigue:

The captain was on deck nearly the whole night, and kept the cook in the galley, with a roaring fire, to make coffee for him, which he took every few hours, and once or twice gave a little to his officers; but not a drop of anything was there for poor Jack. The captain, who sleeps all the daytime, and comes and goes at night as he chooses, can have his brandy and water in the cabin, and his hot coffee at the galley; while Jack, who has to stand through everything, and work in wet and cold, can have nothing to wet his lips or warm his stomach. This was a "temperance ship," and, like too many such ships, the temperance was all in the forecastle. The sailor, who only takes his one glass as it is dealt out to him, is in danger of being drunk; while the captain, who has all under his hand, and can drink as much as he chooses, and upon whose self-possession and cool judgment the lives of all depend, may be trusted with any amount, to drink at his will. (294)

Finally, Dana explains that, when any ship nears home, the crew of nautical Jacks is put to work making her ship-shape and then bright with new paint:

Then, taking two days of calm under the line, we painted her on the outside, giving her open ports in her streak, and finishing off the nice work upon the stern, where sat Neptune in his car, holding his trident, drawn by sea horses; and retouched the gilding and coloring of the cornucopia which ornamented her billet-head. The inside was then painted, from the sky-sail truck to the water-ways . . . The anchors and ring-bolts, and other iron work, were blackened with

129

> coal-tar . . . The cabin, too, is scraped, varnished, and
> painted; and the forecastle scraped and scrubbed; there
> being no need of paint and varnish for Jack's quarters. (335)

Finally, does Dana lighten his tone by conscious puns? He writes of the sailors' dogs: "Welly [named after the Duke of Wellington], at the head, seemed almost to skim over the bushes; and after him came Fanny, Brave, Childers, and the other fleet ones . . ." (157). Having rounded icy Cape Horn homeward-bound, Dana writes truly enough that "Every one was on the alert" (315). A few pages later we read: "Every one was in the highest spirits, and the ship [still the *Alert*] seemed as glad as any of us at getting out of her confinement" (318). Such as they are, these are the only puns in *Two Years Before the Mast;* the absence of others permits the conclusion that these few are unintentional.

II *Myth*

Without much doubt, one reason that *Two Years Before the Mast* appeals to all readers, generation after generation and in many lands, is that its ingredients are elemental, archetypal. It is likely that Dana's masterpiece failed to excite such critics as Maud Bodkin, Joseph Campbell, Richard Chase and S. O. Lesser, among many others who have ignored it, mainly because it has been considered simply juvenile.

Throughout his account, Dana, as a character, betrays deep-seated tensions typical of heroes in many myths. He rushes from his Massachusetts homeland but is sad that he has done so and is most anxious to finish his mission in California and get home again. He is isolated by pride but seeks to be an amiable shipmate and is anxious to learn from older hands and wiser heads. He is relieved when he finds an "immaculate friend"[3] in Ben Stimson, another in the Hawaiian named Hope, then Tom Harris, and finally George Marsh. However, his sense of loneliness is never permanently lifted. Dana was delighted that he could measure up to the challenge of sea duty, he reveled instinctively in the primitive beauties of California, and he rejoiced when he earned the respect of all with whom he came into contact. And yet casting him down constantly was the nagging consciousness that it was wrong for an educated Dana to be starving his mind

and thus betraying his heritage. He becomes almost a legendary
split personality, on the one hand writing frankly and doing dirty
work well, and on the other looking superciliously at his shipmates and apologizing to his readers for his coarse language.
This split is perhaps due to the combination of realistic and
romantic elements in his psychological and literary makeup.

D. H. Lawrence, the only famous critic who has written profoundly about *Two Years Before the Mast,* indicates his awareness of Dana's schizophrenia when he suggests that Dana was
torn between being and knowing. When he simply *felt,* between
the aerial and the watery worlds, he was whole; often he dis-
passionately recorded what he saw, heard, and sensed. But,
Lawrence goes on, when Dana sought to *know* the sea, study
the coastal land, express his outrage at flogging and other in-
justices, then "it was a step . . . in his own undoing. It was a new
phase of dissolution of his own being. Afterwards, he would be
a less human being. He would be a knower: but more near to
mechanism than before."[4] To Lawrence, the true human being
is a romantic; however, Dana the would-be knower was trying
to be a realist.

Much of the "plot" of *Two Years Before the Mast* has mythic
overtones. Like Jason, Aeneas, Parzifal, Gawain, Redburn, Huckleberry Finn, Stephen Dedalus, and many of their brethren, the
hero of *Two Years Before the Mast* leaves home. He is not aided
by his father; in fact, he is opposed by what the father stands for,
which is less than valueless under the new circumstances.[5] He
must pass certain tests to earn entrance into manhood. At one
point he undergoes a rebirth; indeed, his entire experience is a
classic rebirth ritual in its three stages of separation, initiation,
and return.[6] He survives temptations and remains "good" according to his own standards, despite sexual, alcoholic, and other
temptations, and the low example of brutish associates. Although
he is aided by a friend and also feels a little comfort through
being near a surrogate father, his survival is entirely of his own
doing. He even creates his own substitute religion; the old is
behind him and cannot sustain him now, and his new associates
only incompletely accept him. He renews himself, and his belief in
himself, by getting away from everyone and standing on a gaunt,
bare rock. He responds to the basic elements of earth and sea
and sky, using his intelligence and his imagination when he does

so. Finally, just before his successful return and reintegration back home again, he falls victim to a mysterious malady and then to a sense of lassitude, perhaps even to an unvoiced sense that the whole adventure has been full of sound and fury but that it signifies nothing.

In many ways Dana resembles the typical myth hero as synthesized by Professor Joseph Campbell in his *Hero with a Thousand Faces*. Such a hero finds his home confining and his parents conservative; so he responds to the beckoning unknown, only to find new authoritarian restraints which must be destroyed or appeased. The hero is tempted and tested, usually survives, then returns home—changed but now willing to become an authority in his turn.

Notice that Dana voluntarily left a shrunken but still respectable home to cure his eye weakness and also to have an independent adventure. His father, rather like those of Daphne and Brynhild, was a typical restraining parent; but Dana answered the call to danger anyway and left home.[7] On the threshold of his adventure stands Captain Thompson, certainly an archetypal figure of authority, a veritable fire-breathing dragon who, since he cannot be defeated, must be conciliated.[8] Accordingly, our hero obeys every command, even if it is only to hurry up on deck and watch it rain; and he soon may be seen jumping past older sailors to volunteer for hazardous duty. The one time Dana confronts Captain Thompson in deadly opposition, there are mythic overtones. The young man is told that he must stay in the hell of California unless like Admetus he can find a substitute.

Tried and found able on the sea, the hero is more subtly tested ashore. He carries cargo up a hill meaninglessly, like Sisyphus; and, like Psyche and Jason, he also seeks out and carries animal skins reputed to be of great value. With his fellow mariners he wanders into a *pulperia* where debasing wine flows; if we can believe his account, the hero like Ulysses does not turn swinish, nor does he later succumb to any of the local Calypsos. Temptations and other encounters with women, our hero does not mention. It would seem that, like Galahad and Hamlet, he remains pure, at least by his own account.

The hero even has such control over himself that when he and his friends run out of food, through the villainy of the Cyclopean Russell, he can be trusted with their money to go for more:

132

". . . I went up to the town on horseback, with a great salt bag behind the saddle, and a few reáls in my pockets, and brought back the bag full of onions, pears, beans, water-melons, and other fruits; for the young woman [Nausicaa?] who tended the garden, finding that I belonged to the American ship, and that we were short of provisions, put in a double portion" (162).

Dana thinks that he has a helper figure—even a pseudo-father —in the kindly Captain Faucon, who, however, only sits silently by and offers no support in a time of danger. So our hero, standing alone, must draw upon the supernatural protection of his social position and educational background. The name Dana is Achilles' armor, the thread of Ariadne, which protects him and leads him out of the nadir of California to the homeward-bound ship. As he leaves the coast, he knows that he is equal to any challenge on the way back and hence in a sense has experienced his own divinization. Like Prometheus, he has dared to countermand a god's order. He bids farewell to his Olympian crag on the San Juan coast. The Argonauts load the bullock hides and prepare to depart.

The return begins. It is soon marked by an archetypal deluge not of waters but of ice off Cape Horn. It is next notable for the sudden, violent toothache of the hero, which lays him low and forces him off the slippery deck and into the belly of the whale-like ship, in which with the ice grinding outside and seemingly overhead the hero is almost as frightened as Jonah. The vessel finally rounds the Cape after two failures, which have not deterred Thompson, for, we read, "the captain was determined to get round if perseverence could do it, and the third time, he said, never failed" (304). At last the hero is free. The corposant terrifies the others—"Unfortunately, as an omen, it came down" (328) —but it shines upon our hero without adverse effect.

Home again, Dana turned his back but never his mind upon the realms of dream through which he had safely journeyed. He was fearful that perhaps he had lost too much time, even though he had not been gone the dreadful length of time he once feared he might have had to stay in California.[9] Curiously, when safe at home again, he had a dispiriting sense of time lost, like the awakening Rip Van Winkle. Our hero recalled the story of a similar experience told him by a friend, which ended as follows: "Home became almost a dream" (344). Finally, as he stepped

133

RICHARD HENRY DANA, JR.

off the *Alert,* Dana crossed what Professor Campbell calls "the return threshold," thereafter to be "master of the two worlds."[10] Dana had taken a good name and a good mind to sea; he had survived dangers and tests, and had brought a greatly enriched consciousness back home from perilous seas and strange strands. He could now safely resume his studies, perhaps become a lawyer, and strike for justice.

III   *Dana's Book and Other American Journey Books*

Two Years Before the Mast has been a neglected American masterpiece. For, as we have noted, it may be favorably compared with several other American books which also owe their existence to journeys. Washington Irving's *Tour on the Prairies* (1835), telling of his exploration in October, 1832, of east-central Oklahoma west of Fort Gibson, is close to *Two Years Before the Mast* in several ways and was actually finished about the time Dana was visiting Juan Fernandez outward-bound.[11] Some similarities between the two books can be accounted for by the fact that both Irving and Dana went to the wild West for adventure and information. Thus, like Dana, Irving tells us about storms and other elemental dangers, primitive food and loneliness, rude companions and their talk, Indians, impromptu native songs, horses, rattlesnakes, and the like.

But there is much more to the comparison. Both Irving and Dana feel superior to their associates; while they are learning lore and techniques formerly unknown to them, they still refuse to mock at themselves. Both jibe good-naturedly at others, and each indulges in hero worship—Irving with his stalwart half-breed woodsman Pierre Beatte; Dana, with Bill Jackson (90-91). Both writers are pictorial and seem rather "literary" at times, especially Irving, in spite of their avowed intention to be realistic, even debunking, in style. Both use the loglike, diary approach, letting real-life experiences dictate the main outline; however, both vary from strict chronology, especially toward the end, to liven the account with recollected episodes and yarns. Both are slow to report much salty dialogue, although from the few hints they give one may conclude that they heard plenty. The writing of each, while deservedly popular, can be criticized for some carelessness in mechanics and evident haste. Irving has a dozen delightfully dangling participles, gerunds, and infinitives, and he also uses capricious punctuation. But he is far less curious in these respects than Dana.

In several ways *A Tour on the Prairies* is different from *Two Years Before the Mast*. It is more professionally written and is much less gripping. Its tone is more sentimental, since Irving was obviously only having an expensive lark for a month. He remains an uninitiated Eastern tenderfoot, returning to civilization after learning only the most rudimentary lessons of survival in the wilds. Still, it would not be difficult to support the hypothesis that Irving's highly popular book, presenting in thirty-five chapters his departure from civilization, his experiences in primitive conditions, and his return toward a home which at the end seems strange, was an influence upon *Two Years Before the Mast*.

Dana's book in turn was an influence upon several of the works of Herman Melville, who in *White-Jacket* praises various factual accounts of rounding Cape Horn and then adds: "But if you want the best idea of Cape Horn, get my friend Dana's unmatchable 'Two Years Before the Mast.' But you can read, and so you must have read it. His chapters describing Cape Horn must have been written with an icicle."[12] Professor Lucid, who has thoroughly studied the influence of Dana on Melville, demonstrates that "Melville was influenced by Dana's personal suggestions, by a factual voyage narrative [Samuel Leech's *Thirty Years from Home*, 1843] that Dana almost surely recommended, and finally by a whole genre which Dana was influential in popularizing."[13] Then Lucid convincingly shows Dana's influence on Melville's treatment of many characters and incidents in *Redburn* and *White-Jacket*.[14] Since Melville read *Two Years Before the Mast* shortly before leaving America aboard the *Acushnet* in December, 1840,[15] it is likely that *Typee* (1846) and *Omoo* (1847), as well as *Redburn* (1849) and *White-Jacket* (1850), also owe something to Dana.

In form, *Typee, Omoo,* and *Redburn* are similar to *Two Years Before the Mast*. Each is a three-part work. *Typee* concerns unpleasant life aboard a real ship, then Tommo's bittersweet island life, and finally his escape to his own kind again. Thus its structure slightly resembles that of Dana's book. Each work features a heartless sea captain, a close friend for the hero, and sexual situations necessarily veiled.

In *Omoo* the three-part structure appears again. The first part tells of unbearable (though often comical) life aboard ship. The next section concerns Omoo's life in and around the Tahitian *calabooza* (Dana spells its California equivalent "calabozo"). The last part details Omoo's picaresque wanderings through the islands in the company of Dr. Long Ghost, an unimmaculate friend whose background somewhat resembles those of Dana's friends Tom Harris and George Marsh. *Omoo* is also like *Two Years Before the Mast* in other ways: Jermin countermands his ineffectual captain's orders as promptly if not so tactfully as Wilson does Thompson's in San Diego Harbor. We have accurately reported Kanaka talk in both books. And Melville is hardly more bitter toward the Christian missionaries in the Pacific area than Dana is toward Yankee commercialism in California.

Redburn also has a three-part structure close to that of *Two Years Before the Mast*. The first part tells of Redburn's misery as the lad leaves home and sails across the Atlantic Ocean to Liverpool; next we have his Liverpool and London observations; then follows his relatively mature return home. There are other similarities, in addition to such parallel specific incidents, which Lucid reports, as the initial naïveté of Dana and Redburn, their seasickness, their first unpleasant sea duty aloft, their joy at seeing other ships at sea, the anomalous position of their second mates, and their hearing whales breathing in the foggy night.[16] Both Redburn and Dana suffer under vicious captains and unpleasant working and living conditions; and each finds an immaculate friend, whom he loses. Each book recounts the initiation of the central youth to an awareness of evil at sea and ashore; each is marked by the incident of a fall to death in the water; and each is carelessly written at times.

Of course, *Redburn*, like *Typee* and *Omoo*, is different from *Two Years Before the Mast* in ways too numerous to need summarizing. Lucid aptly concludes: "As *Redburn* develops, it moves away from the kind of material used by Dana, but it appears that Melville referred to Dana's book in his search for appropriate detail to make vivid the initial experiences of a green hand."[17]

Concerning duty on a man-of-war, cast entirely at sea, and in addition didactic at many points, *White-Jacket* is not basically like Dana's book. However, Melville's mythic male ideal here is Jack Chase, and his characteristics may owe something to Dana's Bill Jackson, "the thoroughbred English sailor" (90) whom Dana glimpsed briefly and never forgot. (Curiously, Melville named Redburn's most villainous shipmate Jackson.) Details of rounding Cape Horn, whether aboard the *Neversink* or the *Alert,* are necessarily similar. And so with such details as holystones, prayerbooks, frozen rigging, moonlight on pyramidal sails, and the halfbitter, half-comic talk of seamen longing for the land.[18]

Melville is most strikingly different from Dana for exaggerating various routine incidents for the sake of vivid effect. Thus, Dana gets through the time of his greenness with fewer mishaps and jeers than Redburn. Dana hears the common sailors called "the people" (14) but makes less of it satirically than Melville does in *White-Jacket.* When Forster asks leave and is brusquely refused, Dana reports the matter and then drops it; Melville humorously exaggerates Jack Chase's successful appeal to Captain Claret for leave. When Dana witnesses the flogging of Sam and John, he is as sickened as Melville but restrains his emotions and his pen better. Dana's farewell to Hope, the Hawaiian, is as moving as Redburn's to Harry Bolton, but it occupies less space and is more realistically reported. Both authors discuss the antiwhaling sentiment then existing aboard merchant vessels, but Melville plays it up for more comedy. Finally, Redburn's knowledge of the passengers' doings on his return trip is hard to credit; Dana more honestly says simply that he cannot talk much with Professor Nuttall.

It might be concluded that Melville in these voyage novels was working toward *Moby Dick* with its poetically exaggerated depiction of violence and depravity, whereas Dana is content with the more prosaic task of picturing routine work at sea and along the coast. With Melville the sea became an ambivalent metaphor; with Dana it stays a literal medium.

Francis Parkman and his *Oregon Trail* (1849) are similar in many ways to Dana and his book. A snobbish and conservative Bostonian, a graduate of Harvard and its law school, and later a hard-driving master of his specialty, Parkman went west in 1846 to St. Louis and then Wyoming, seeking adventure and information of historical value. He also sought to improve his eyesight and general health. (In this search he failed, unlike Dana). Serialized in 1847, Parkman's book was published two years later under a title as misleading as Dana's; it was called *The California and Oregon Trail.*

The Oregon Trail is somewhat like *Two Years Before the Mast* in structure; and Parkman's handling of incidents, descriptions, rhetorical problems, humor, and tone are even closer to Dana's. Although he treats his departure from St. Louis and Fort Leavenworth and his return to Leavenworth more sketchily than Dana does his voyages, Parkman still employs a similar three-part structure. The first three chapters of this twenty-seven-chapter book are preliminary to his "Jumping Off" for Fort Laramie and the Ogillallah village, which is Parkman's Cape Horn-like destination and is described in the middle chapter (Chapter XIV) of his book. The two-chapter return is swift: "Down the Arkansas" to "The Settlements." So we have a 3-22-2-chapter structure. Like Dana, Parkman combines a loose chronological movement, made clear by occasional journal-like dates, with anecdotes and little informational essays. Like Irving, Dana, and Twain, he also includes splendidly graphic descriptions of natural scenes. And, like Irving and Dana, he scatters evenly through his narrative numerous dangling modifiers and outmoded double negatives. He also repeats his introductions of persons and delays his definitions of terms—for example, *shongsasha*. He awkwardly switches to the present tense, as Dana does occasionally in *Two Years Before the Mast* and with exasperating frequency in *To Cuba and Back*. Both authors quote Shakespeare and mention Sir Walter Scott. Both use infrequent dialogue with some effectiveness. Parkman's equivalent of Dana's ironic "pleasant" (meaning "unpleasant") is "agreeable" (meaning "disagreeable" or "not agreeable").

More important than similarities in style is the similar tone which Dana and Parkman adopt in their books. Both are willing to poke fun often at the plights and deficiencies of others, less often at their own. Both are conscious of their Eastern superiority. Each wants it understood that his journey is but an episode in a life destined for better things. Each extols a stalwart natural ideal—Parkman's equivalent of Dana's Bill Jackson is the superb hunter Henry Chatillon. And curiously, each is dragged down by a malady—somewhat like Tommo's infected leg in *Typee*. Dana's toothache become Parkman's debilitating dysentery. Finally, like *Two Years Before the Mast*, *The Oregon Trail* rewards those who seek elements which contribute to myth-reading. The major difference between the two men is that Parkman went on to write better books, whereas Dana never outdid his youthful work.

Thoreau once wrote, "I have traveled a good deal in Concord."[19] His saunters there and around Walden Pond nearby resulted in one of the most remarkable quest metaphors in world literature—*Walden* (1854). When Dana returned to Harvard, he was permitted to join and ultimately to graduate with the class of 1837, which included Henry David Thoreau. Two personalities more different could not easily be imagined. Dana was conservative; Thoreau, radical. Dana was snobbishly and seriously aristocratic; Thoreau humbly and humorously numbered all of God's creatures among his friends. Dana revered the Constitution; Thoreau recognized "Higher Laws." Dana lived to regard his fast-written *Two Years Before the Mast* as a boy's work; Thoreau poured the treasures of a brief lifetime of thought and action into his slowly evolved *Walden*.

Yet in several ways the two books are similar. The 2-14-2-chapter structure of *Walden* is reminiscent of Dana's 8-20-8 form. Both authors follow the cycles of nature—Dana by echoing such rhythms as departure-initiation-return and sea-land-sea; Thoreau by patterning his work after the rhythm of spring through to spring again, and also death and rebirth. Both books have pairs of contrasting chapters which contribute to similar arch effects. Note, for example, Thoreau's I-XVIII and VI-XIV pairs, and the thematically central Chapter XI—"Higher Laws." (Thoreau, however, in addition builds a contrapuntal rhythm with successive chapters which are contrasting, for example V then VI, and VII then VIII.)[20]

Both authors are romantic about nature and natural things. Dana's response to the ocean and the remote coast is poetic, much like Thoreau's response to the deep forest, though Dana is far less philosophical. Dana admired the natural goodness of the Hawaiians and his good dog Bravo; Thoreau revered the Indians and sympathized with the harried fox. Each went to nature for reductive, educative purposes. While willingly placing themselves amid natural beauty, they both escaped it by reading, as indeed Parkman did at Fort Laramie and Ernest Hemingway did in East Africa. Both Dana and Thoreau were stimulated by nature to recall literary lines, including Latin ones. We may legitimately view the experience of both as archetypally heroic and regenerative. Nonetheless, it should be repeated that Episcopal Dana and

Transcendental Thoreau are poles apart in most respects. Their books may be superficially similar in several interesting ways; however, Thoreau was a brilliant professional writer and a self-reliant naturalist, whereas Dana was basically something quite different.[21]

Mark Twain dismays those who try to compare him with others. But *Roughing It* (1871) and "Old Times on the Mississippi" (1875) resemble *Two Years Before the Mast* in significant ways. *Roughing It* is a more thorough presentation of the American dream than *Two Years Before the Mast* is, since it has three basic ingredients—the beckoning West, native innocence, and rags-to-riches[22]—whereas Dana turns his back on the last two. Unlike Dana's book, *Roughing It* has no discernible structure. The first volume is evenly divided into two parts, the first telling of Twain's getting to Nevada, and the second describing various episodes there. The second volume is unevenly given over to accounts of Twain's journalistic career in the West, his visit to Hawaii, and then his trip back to California. Twain asymmetrically fails to return to his point of departure, which separates him from Irving, Dana, much of Melville, Parkman, and Thoreau.

But, like Dana and others, Twain shows us a neophyte becoming a veteran.[23] As a tenderfoot, he deserves as much self-spoofing as any of the other writers under discussion, but Twain is unique in heaping humorous abuse on himself; only Melville comes close. Twain is also unequaled in reporting native dialogue and is among the best—as is Dana—at describing fresh Western scenery. Like Dana too, Twain skirts a few chances to be frank about loose morals in that virgin land. Again like Dana, Twain is indignant at the white man's propensity to victimize migrant elements on the Pacific coast: Dana sides with the Kanaka against the whites; Twain, with the Chinese against them.

"Old Times on the Mississippi"[24] is different in structure from Dana's work. It is a one-part nostalgic tone poem. But it resembles *Two Years Before the Mast* in being the story of a cub initiated into a sailing process. And Twain here is like Irving, Dana, Parkman, and even Thoreau in painting a wondrous part of America not yet ruined by commercialism. He also has his male ideal, although a partly comic one, in the redoubtable steamboat pilot Horace Bixby, to match Pierre Beatte, Bill Jackson, Toby, Dr. Long Ghost, Harry Bolton, Jack Chase, Henry Chatillon, and Hemingway's Jackson "Pop" Phillips.

It is a long leap to 1935 and *Green Hills of Africa*,[25] but no American writer between Twain and Hemingway has produced a book much like the curious combination of ingredients which *Two Years Before the Mast* is. Indeed, Ernest Hemingway's avowed purpose in *Green Hills of Africa* reads like a little preface to Dana's book if one merely makes a couple of simple substitutions: "Unlike many novels, none of the characters or incidents in this book is imaginary. Any one not finding sufficient love interest is at liberty, while reading it, to insert whatever love interest he or she may have at the time. The writer has attempted to write an absolutely true book to see whether the shape of a country and the pattern of a month's action can, if truly presented, compete with a work of the imagination."[26]

In form the two books are similar. Hemingway divided his into four parts, with a 2-7-2-2-chapter structure. But it might as easily be 2-9-2, since Parts II and III deal with memories of unsatisfactory hunting and with present failures. The first two chapters lead us into the hunting expedition; the last two, to resounding successes.

Other comparisons are notable. Like Dana, Hemingway had been sick—with amoebic dysentery—before he started on his adventure; and travel invigorated him quickly, as it did Dana. Hemingway loves the new country he sees and deplores the inevitability of its being commercially exploited. He admires his native gun-bearers and trackers as much as Dana does the hide-bearing, nautical Kanakas. Hemingway sets a high standard for himself: he takes pride in mastering the ritual of the hunt, doing more than his share, earning the commendation of Pop and the admiration of M'Cola, learning a little Swahili, and commenting on items in his bookbag, which is somewhat like Dana's sea-chest. He tosses about native lingo and hunting terms the way Dana does Spanish, Kanaka, and sea jargon. Dana's love of such names as Monterey, Catalina, and San Diego, which were names of faraway places then, resembles Hemingway's well-known adoration of place names: in *Green Hills of Africa* we have Babati, Handeni, Kondoa-Irangi, Nairobi, and the Rift Valley. The Rift Valley reminds Hemingway of Wyoming, just as San Juan reminds Dana of Nahant and Newport.

Both writers sometimes indulge in subtle humor, usually at the expense of others.[27] Obviously, *Green Hills of Africa* is the lighter, happier book of the two. Hemingway is mostly having fun

RICHARD HENRY DANA, JR.

which time is shaping fore and aft, whereas Dana for the most part is going through danger and drudgery which time seems inordinately slow in terminating. Hemingway has the companionship of his wife P. O. M. (Poor Old Mama), which permits a few lightly risqué passages of the sort Dana felt obliged to avoid rigorously. Finally, it may be remarked that both authors seek to reproduce the exact sense of specific events, and in forms dictated by real time. As Professor Carlos Baker states when writing of *Green Hills of Africa*, "The two major aspects of the experiment are the attempt at verisimilitude ('the shape of a country') and architectonics ('the pattern of a month's action')."[28] He might well have been commenting on Dana's literary experiment.[29]

Two Years Before the Mast, then, resembles several other American travel and initiation accounts, most notably *Redburn, The Oregon Trail, Roughing It,* and *Green Hills of Africa.* It is like some of them in narrative techniques and in structure; like others in matters of composition, tone, attitudes, and incidents. Dana in fundamental ways is different both as a man and as an author from Melville, Parkman, Thoreau, Twain, and Hemingway. But his work, like theirs, fits into an archetypal story mold —that of the willing quester through enigmatic nature.

CHAPTER 8

Other Works

IN SPITE OF his genuine literary talent, Dana unfortunately wrote relatively few works in addition to his *Two Years Before the Mast*. Had his professional and political duties not consumed his time and energy for decades, he surely would have followed his manual on seamanship and his travel book on Cuba with more books. After his retirement, his projected treatise on international law and his ambitious plans for an autobiography and a Dana family history were abruptly canceled by his sudden death in Rome. All the same, his minor works include *The Seaman's Friend, To Cuba and Back,* and *Speeches in Stirring Times and Letters to a Son*. And, in lieu of an autobiography, his intriguing *Journal* is a highly satisfactory substitute.

I The Seaman's Friend (*1841*)

The full title of this popular and readable little book explains its comprehensive purpose: *The Seaman's Friend; Containing a Treatise on Practical Seamanship, with Plates; a Dictionary of Sea Terms; Customs and Usages on the Merchant Service; Laws Relating to the Practical Duties of Master and Mariners* (the book was published in London by Edward Moxon as *The Seaman's Manual*). Tactfully dedicated to all seafaring persons— especially greenhorns—to shipowners and insurers, to maritime judges and lawyers, and to all other interested persons, this handbook is divided into three parts: practical seamanship, including a fascinating dictionary of sea terms; merchant-service customs and usages; and laws relating to masters, officers, crew members, and passengers. Included are five plates, illustrating spars and rigging, basic types of sailing vessels, and basic knots.
The book is a model of logical organization. The first part begins with the construction of vessels, their weights and mea-

surements, ballast and lading. It then discusses rigging, masts and yards, sails, and blocks and purchases. Next it considers making and taking in sail, working a ship generally, how to respond to gales and accidents, and how to anchor and get under way. For the convenience of landlubberly readers, Dana places his nautical glossary at the end of this part. Linguists and inquisitive readers in general should take pleasure in this thirty-five-page dictionary, with its definitions of such intriguing words and phrases as the following, among many others: *a-cock-bill, becket, box-hauling, bum-boat, burton, cat-harpin, cat's-paw, chapelling, chess-trees, clew-garnet, cuckold's neck, dead-eye, dolphin-striker, eupluve, fid, fother, garboard-streak, goring-clothes, hogged, keckling, lizard, nippers, parliament-heel, paunch mat, pink-stern, puddening, sister block, snotter, spoon-drift, surge ho!, syphering, tail-tackle, timenoguy, vang, wind-rode,* and *wing-and-wing.*

Part Two tells of the responsibilities of the master, then the chief mate, and then the second and third mates. Next it describes the duties of carpenter, sailmaker, steward, cook, able seaman, ordinary seaman, and so on down to green hands and mere boys. A miscellaneous chapter concerns watches, bells, discipline, food, and the like.

The last part is a thoroughly documented little maritime-law textbook, with every page footnoted by references to pertinent laws, cases, and reports. This part was perhaps the most valuable section of the book for contemporary readers, especially ordinary seamen anxious to know their duties and legal rights. It begins with laws about the vessel itself and its equipment; then the master's relation to ship, cargo, passengers, officers, and crew members; the privileges and duties of passengers, and then those of the officers. The entire second half of this part is devoted to seamen, with respect to contracts, desertion or absence, sickness, rights and protection, punishment, revolt and mutiny, piracy, wages, and procedures to follow in suing.

Dana's little book may sound dull, but it is not. If we make allowance for the technical vocabulary, the treatise is crystal-clear and engagingly informative. Dana's detailed table of contents quickly enables any reader to find everything he needs to know. For example, a sailor who happened to buy Dana's book to learn how to recover wages due him but withheld could rapidly do so, and in addition read footnoted citations to eight cases or precedents in the bargain.

The style of Dana's treatise is simple. His purpose is to explain complicated techniques, relationships, and responsibilities as fully and sensibly as possible. At no time does Dana parade his own experiences, look down his nose at his readers, or get literary. The resulting manual has a distinct if subdued charm, like that of a simple, functional artifact. *The Seaman's Friend* succeeds admirably in its purpose; but devotees of *Two Years Before the Mast* will look in vain for personal anecdotes or gripping narrative in this book. For example, in discussing "Man Overboard," Dana remains dispassionate and professional, though it is to be assumed that he remembered poor George Ballmer as he wrote about procedures to follow in trying to rescue a lost sailor.

The very dispassionateness of Dana's wording throughout *The Seaman's Friend* is curiously exciting. Readers who know *Two Years Before the Mast* may find much interesting material in this follow-up, which in some ways is an unemotional obverse to it.

II To Cuba and Back: A Vacation Voyage (*1859*)

The hastily composed account by Dana of his twelve busy days of touring in Cuba, which he called *To Cuba and Back: A Vacation Voyage* and published within two months of his return in March, 1859, is a spotty but interesting document.

It is divided into twenty-five chapters. The first three describe Dana's voyage to Havana by steamer; the last two tell of his trip back to New York. All but one of the middle twenty chapters relate in simple chronological order, with no flourishes of style, his sight-seeing and close observation of social, religious, economic, political, and cultural institutions in Havana, Matanzas, and Limonar. Chapter XXIII, the most efficiently informative, is a catch-all of little essays on Cuban politics, religion, slavery, natural resources, and education. The most chilling chapters, XI-XIV, describe various phases of slave life on a huge sugar plantation near Limonar. Chapter XX is by far the most humorous: it pictures the Havana bullfight almost as wittily and sarcastically as James Russell Lowell, author of *The Biglow Papers*, or Mark Twain, author of "The Horse's Tail," might have done it.

The weakness of the rest of the book lies in its relentless parade of facts and figures, which make apparent the author's distance from his subject. For example, Dana refuses to be indignant regarding slavery at the Chartrand *ingenio,* because he prefers to be a proper guest of his aristocratic host. Apparently feeling that he owes it to his readers, Dana asks to see the garrote at the Havana prison, but is refused.[1] And he goes to the bullfight in spite of his prejudice against it. "Shall we go? I would not, if it were only pleasure that I was seeking. As I am sure I expect only the contrary, and wish merely to learn the character of the national recreation, I will go" (197).*

Dana strikes a clever balance between the "innocent abroad" and the "passionate pilgrim." For an example of the former, does not the following anticipate Twain almost at his best? "If mosquito nets were invented for the purpose of shutting mosquitoes in with you, they answer their purpose very well. The beds have no mattresses, and you lie on the hard sacking. This favors coolness and neatness. I should fear a mattress, in the economy of our hotel, at least. Where there is nothing but an iron frame, canvas stretched over it, and sheets and a blanket, you may know what you are dealing with" (51). Or Dana's really delightful handling of the bullfight? Enter the matador:

> . . . a fierce-looking fellow, dressed in dark green, with a large head of curling, snaky black hair, and a skin almost black. He makes a great strut and flourish, and after two or three unsuccessful attempts to get the bull head on, at length, getting a fair chance, plunges his black sword to the hilt in the bull's neck,—but there is no fall of the bull. He has missed the spinal cord, and the bull trots off, bleeding in a small stream, with a sword-handle protruding a few inches above the hide of his back-neck. The spectators hoot their contempt for the failure; but with no sign of pity for the beast. The bull is weakened, but trots about and makes a few runs at cloths, and the sword is drawn from his hide by an agile dart-sticker . . . and given to the black bully in dark green, who makes one more lunge, with no better success. (202-3)

---

* All parenthetical references in this section are to Richard Henry Dana, Jr., *To Cuba and Back: A Vacation Voyage* (Boston, 1859).

After the first bull is finally killed, we read the following: "Shall I stay another? Perhaps it may be more successful, and—if the new bull will only bruise somebody! But the new bull is a failure" (203). Finally we read that the sixth bull

> . . . gores one horse a little,—the horse standing, side on, and taking it, until the bull is driven off by the punching of the spear; and runs at the other horse, and, to my delight, upsets the rider, but unfortunately without hurting him, and the black-haired matador in green tries his hand on him and fails again, and is hooted, and takes to throwing darts, and gets a fall, and looks disconcerted, and gets his sword again, and makes another false thrust; and the crippled and bleeding animal is thrown down and dispatched by the butcher with his short knife, and drawn off by the three poor horses. The gates close, and I hurry out of the theatre, in a din of shouts and drums and trumpets, the great crowd waiting for the last bull;—but I have seen enough. (205-06)

Perhaps the critical "innocent" had had enough, but never the "passionate pilgrim." Dana's book overflows with devoted observations of natural and man-made beauty in Cuba: "There indeed is the Morro, a stately hill of tawny rock, rising perpendicularly from the sea, and jutting into it, with walls and parapets and towers on its top, and flags and signals flying, and the tall lighthouse just in front of its outer wall" (27).

Looking at the beautiful setting of Havana, Dana quotes his favorite lines from Bryant's "Thanatopsis" about "Old Ocean's gray and melancholy waste" and then passionately adds, "No! Not so! Young Ocean, the Ocean of to-day! Young Ocean, the Ocean of to-day! The blue, bright, healthful, glittering, gladdening, inspiring Ocean! Have I ever seen a city view so grand? The view of Quebec from the foot of the Montmorenci [*sic*] Falls, may rival, but does not excel it. My preference is for this . . ." (66). When he approaches the Havana Cathedral, he is equally enraptured:

> The Cathedral, in its exterior, is a plain and quaint old structure, with a tower at each angle of the floor; but within, it is sumptuous. There is a floor of variegated marble, obstructed by no seats or screens, tall pillars and rich frescoed walls, and delicate masonry of various colored stones, the prevailing

147

tint being yellow, and a high altar of porphyry. There is a look of the great days of Old Spain about it; and you think that knights and nobles worshipped here and enriched it from their spoils and conquests. (55-56)

But Dana does not let the glitter of the sea and the pale glow of church marble blind him to the tragic rottenness spreading through Cuba like a stain. He thoroughly appraises the whole Cuban system, and his book reflects his complex intellectual, rhetorical, and emotional response. Temperately suggesting that the ethnic, political, and social fabric of Cuba is a tangle, he concludes that the outsider simply cannot understand it. But he can put searching questions:

> Shall the industry of Cuba go on, or shall the island be abandoned to a state of nature? If the former, and if the whites cannot do the hard labor in the climate, and the blacks can, will the seven hundred thousand whites, who own all the land and improvements, surrender them to the blacks and leave the island, or will they remain? If they must be expected to remain, what is to be the relation of the two races? The blacks must do the hard work, or it will not be done. Shall it be the enforced labor of slavery, or shall the experiment of free labor be tried? Will the government try the experiment, and if so, on what terms and in what manner? If something is not done by the government, slavery will continue; for a successful insurrection of slaves in Cuba is impossible, and manumissions do not gain upon the births and importations. (257-58)

Available facts lead Dana to the dour prediction that one "may well be slow to believe that, with their complication of difficulties, and causes of disorder and weakness, the Cubans will work out successfully the problem of self-government" (267-68).[2] Dana can at least find relief in penning this silent rhetorical rebuke to the shouting maniacs at the bull slaughter and elsewhere:

> You can cry and howl at bull-fights and cock-fights and in the pits of operas and theatres, and drive bulls and horses distracted, and urge gallant game-cocks to the death and applaud opera singers into patriotic songs, and leave them to imprisonment and fines [*I Puritani* singers were ordered

> to substitute *Leatà* for *Libertà*],—and you yourselves, cannot
> lift a finger, or join hand to hand, or bring to the hazard life,
> fortune, or honor, for your liberty and your dignity as men.
> Work your slaves, torture your bulls, fight your game-cocks,
> crown your dancers and singers,—and leave the weightier
> matters of judgment and justice, fame by sea and land, of
> letters and arts and sciences, of private right and public
> honor, the present and future of your race and of your native
> land, to the care of others,—of a people of no better blood
> than your own, strangers and sojourners among you! (204-5)

Finally, Dana expresses an emotional response when, on the
morning of his departure, he again sees the plodding chain
gang: "I shall not see them again, but there they will be, day
after day, day after day,—how long?—aye, how long?—the squalid,
degraded chain-gang! The horrible prison!—profaning one of
the grandest of sites, where city, sea and shore unite as almost
nowhere else on earth! These were my thoughts as, in the pink
and gray dawn, I walked down the Paseo, to enjoy my last refreshing in the rock-hewn sea-baths" (273).

In spite of many good passages, *To Cuba and Back* is far inferior to *Two Years Before the Mast*. Dana is only an observant
alien visiting Cuba for less than two weeks and knowing that he
will soon be gone. Stylistically, *To Cuba and Back* is flawed like
Two Years Before the Mast by quotas of dangling modifiers
("Pressing this upon an intelligent ecclesiast, his reply to me
was . . ." [242]); affected double or near-double negatives ("At
break of day, I am in the delightful sea-baths again, not ill-named
Recreo and Elíseo" [179]); and slipshod punctuation.

In addition, Dana annoyingly adopts a basic present tense
throughout most of the book. Occasionally he slips into the past
tense, but for the most part only briefly. All but four chapters
start in the present tense. Sometimes this device is rather effective, as in Chapter XI, when Dana first shows us the sugar
plantation: we feel not only that we are there but also that the
victimized slaves are perhaps still there. However, the sudden
shifts in tense to the past often seem pretentious and illogical,
and they are usually bewildering. The following is a simple example of one such exasperating shift in a single paragraph: "To-
night there is again a mascare at the next door, but my room is
now more remote, and I am able to sleep through it. Once I

awoke. It was nearly five o'clock. The music was still going on
. . . The drums and trumpets were hushed, and all had fallen . . .
into a trance of sound, a rondo of constantly returning delicious
melody . . . It is a contradanza of Cuba. The great bells beat
five, . . . and instantly the music ceases . . ." (178).

Perhaps better than *Two Years Before the Mast* in one respect,
To Cuba and Back has a clever little pattern of nautical similes
and metaphors. One of the most effective is a brilliant metaphor
contrasting Cuba with America at the time of the Revolution:

> The thirteen colonies were ships fully armed and equipped,
> officered and manned, with long sea experience, sailing as
> wing of a great fleet, under the Admiral's fleet signals. They
> had only to pass secret signals, fall out of line, haul their
> wind, and sail off as a squadron by themselves; and if the
> Admiral with the rest of the fleet made chase and gave
> battle, it was sailor to sailor and ship to ship. But Cuba has
> neither officers trained to the quarter-deck, nor sailors trained
> to the helm, the yard, or the gun. Nay, the ship is not built,
> nor the keel laid, nor is the timber grown, from which the
> keel is to be cut. (268-69)

Dana's report of Yankee dialogue overhead on the bus leaving
the bullfight is worthy of his friend James Russell Lowell. By
means of this humorous dialogue, which is too long to be quoted,
Dana can get in his digs against the Cubans and yet stand aside,
if need be, and with a straight face disclaim any responsibility.
In conception and execution, the device anticipates Twain.

Finally, in his uneven but never dull book Dana brilliantly
describes how the sugar-plantation workers crush the canestalks
and boil them into marketable material. The magnificent word
picture is long and detailed, and it ends philosophically in a way
which perhaps pleased the author of "The Try-Works," Chapter
XCVI of *Moby Dick*:

> Thus, on one side of the roller is the ceaseless current of
> fresh, full, juicy cane-stalks, just cut from the open field;
> and on the other side, is the crushed, mangled, juiceless
> mass, drifting out at the draught, and fit only to be cast into
> the oven and burned. This is the way of the world, as it is
> the course of art. The cane is made to destroy itself. The
> ruined and corrupted furnish the fuel and fan the flame that
> lures on and draws in and crushes the fresh and wholesome;

and the operation seems about as mechanical and unceasing in the one case as in the other. (125-26)

III *Speeches and Letters*

The assorted Dana material compiled by his devoted son and published in 1910 as *Speeches in Stirring Times and Letters to a Son* is obviously two books in one. It contains thirteen of Dana's most effective speeches and essays, and in addition it presents the most extensive collection of Dana letters to date—some sixty, or parts thereof, to his son. Both the speeches and the letters should make any reader wish that he had ready access to more of them, especially more of the speeches.

Dana was a brilliant orator, marshaling great stores of erudition with rare logic and force. His son draws a valuable word picture of him in action: "I can see him now, short (he was only five feet seven inches in height), erect, with square, broad shoulders, a graceful figure, with small hands and feet, curling hair and elastic step, walking up and down the room, his head a little to one side, his eyes slightly raised, thinking out some problem, or developing the arguments in its support."[3] Dana was also, as we have already seen, a vigorous if usually too conservative and serious letter writer.

Speeches in Stirring Times

In "The Bible in Schools," Dana defends a Maine school committee from a suit by a Roman Catholic father for its exclusion of his son from school because of the boy's refusal to read the King James version of the Bible rather than the Douay. Predictably, Dana argues for tradition, law, and morality. Of special charm are his comments on the Bible, which it would be unreasonable to banish because of a few controversially translated passages, omitted from school reading anyway. The law requires schools to provide moral training, which must be based—says Dana—upon religion. Hence the Bible is used, and properly the King James version because the United States is an English-speaking country proud of its Anglo-Saxon heritage. Everyone who speaks English should study this version anyway, since it is a literary treasure.

In "Speech on the Judiciary; Massachusetts Constitutional Con-

vention of 1853," Dana eloquently argues against a proposal
to have judges either elected by the people or appointed by the
government for specific terms. Dana contends that, if the people
elected them, they would be swept into and out of office on the
whims of tyrannous changing majorities. If appointed for fixed
periods, they would have to appeal to the executive for reap-
pointment and thus become an aspect of political patronage.
Like Alexis de Tocqueville, Dana inveighs against the majority;
and, anticipating by almost three decades the intellectuals behind
the Pendleton Civil Service Act, he heatedly vilifies the spoils
system. Finally, he lectures the assembled delegates on the advantages of the American system of checks and balances, and
then praises the farseeing wisdom of our Constitution's writers
who wanted judges "as free, impartial and independent as the lot
of humanity will admit" (84).*

In this generally splendid speech Dana is too anxious to parade
his erudition and to demonstrate his talent for lightning-quick
response. Still, most of the listeners must have been delighted[4]
by the informative, captivating speech, with its rhetorical questions, skillful forensic logic, occasional light sarcasm, graphic
imagery, and combination of modesty and mock-modesty. Pleading for retention of the present healthy judicial system, Dana
offers a really convincing analogy: ". . . it is bad enough to see
two surgeons sitting by the side of a sick man, quarreling between themselves what they will do with him; but to have them
seize hold of a man in health, and bind him hand and foot, to try
experiments upon him, and not to be able to agree what they
shall do to him! that is cruelty as well as folly. And yet, Sir, that
is precisely the state of things here" (115).

In "Usury Laws, February 14, 1867," Dana as a member of the
Massachusetts Legislature is effective if somewhat long-winded.
The speech is based on his belief in laissez-faire and the efficacy
of the old law of supply and demand, if unfettered. Giving a little
history of usury laws, he says that, although they were once
noble, they are now outmoded, and adds that most enlightened
centers of capital have repealed them with no ill effects. Dana's
main argument is that, since the value of money fluctuates in

* All parenthetical references in this section are to Richard Henry Dana,
Jr., *Speeches in Stirring Times and Letters to a Son* (Boston, 1910).

accordance with supply and demand, it is unwise to fix the market rate of interest by law. By way of conclusion, he suggests that, at present, bank holdings available for loans are swelled by savings accounts of innumerable solvent workers, and that the big borrowers are contractors and corporations.

The speech is marred by a trace of anti-Semitism and a measure of naïveté. In saying that under usury laws, "the Jews emerge from their alleys, and the curb-stone brokers swarm" (135), Dana seems to forget that loan sharks come from all races and creeds. Further, in criticizing the contractor who "builds those large blocks of houses, too costly for you or me, sir, to live in, and sells them for prices that we cannot afford to pay" (141), he appears to turn his back on the sacred law of supply and demand. But the oration is generally excellent: it is erudite, eloquent, and logical.

"Free Soil Meeting, in 1848, at Boston: Remarks on Taking the Chair at the Free Soil Meeting, at the Tremont Temple, Friday Evening, July 7, 1848" was Dana's first important political speech; and it is short, gloomily idealistic, and prophetic. At the outset Dana stresses his youth and ingrained conservatism, saying that he used to be a Whig of the old school who, ever since he began voting in 1840, has supported Whig candidates. But, like other young Whigs, he has become alarmed by the recent nomination of Zachary Taylor as the Whig candidate for President, because it is a triumph for the South and because Northern indifference to it is an abandonment of the principles of the Free Soilers. He urges men of Massachusetts to return to their traditional opposition to the extension of slavery into new territory. He closes with an appeal to "the right reason and right feeling of the people" (148).

"Buffalo Free Soil Convention, 1848: Speech at Faneuil Hall, August 22, 1848: Reporting the Doings of the Buffalo Convention, in Behalf of the Boston Delegation" is a simple informational speech (repeated in several Massachusetts cities) in which Dana reports on the Free Soil Convention held in Buffalo. Dana first presents some background information on the various parties, all of whom were united by a common sacred goal. After reporting how Charles Francis Adams was elected to preside over the Convention and how a platform committee met to enunciate the Free Soilers' principles, Dana summarizes the positions of the leading candidates and explains how former President Martin Van Buren was nominated, even though he was a Democrat. "Of all the prominent Whig statesmen, there was not one willing to put himself upon our Convention, and abide the issue of our cause,—no, not one. If there is a Whig in Faneuil who doubts . . . , let him name . . . a single Whig statesman of the first class, fit to be the head of our party, whom we could have put in nomination, or let him forever after hold his peace" (157). Dana closes by explaining that, after the unanimous nomination of Van Buren, the Western delegates, granted the privilege of naming the vice-presidential candidate, nominated Charles Francis Adams with riotous and unanimous enthusiasm.[5]

"The Great Gravitation Meeting" is Dana's only satirical "speech" (it was published, not delivered), and it is a dismal one. The deadpan assumption is that persons born in the Southern hemisphere but living in the North should be returned to the South whenever Southerners feel that it would endanger the gravitation or equilibrium of the earth to leave such persons in the North. The principal defender of this Law of Gravitation is Daniel Webster, and his fictitious speech in Boston is witheringly reported. It includes the following: "As for me, my part is taken. Standing here in Faneuil Hall, with Bunker Hill before me, with Lexington and Concord on my left hand, and the Rock of Plymouth on my right, I give my heart and hand for this law" (171).

Obviously, for the Law of Gravitation Dana's readers would substitute the Fugitive Slave Law; for Northern hemisphere, Northern states; and for Southern hemisphere, slave states. But Dana's son calls the satirical piece a "parody on the Fugitive Slave Law for the 'preservation' of the United States Constitution ('gravitation') with its slavery compromises"[6] Obviously, when Dana describes with mock-seriousness the need to preserve the earth's equilibrium by shifting Southerners back where they came from, he is satirizing Southern determination to drag back escaped slaves. He may even be prophetically flirting with the later well-credited theory that a better course of action for the South would have been to forget the tiny minority of slaves who made good their escape to the North. But Dana is hardly equating the man-made Constitution, including its built-in provision for amendments, with the divine, immutable law of gravity.

"Argument on Behalf of Charles G. Davis, Esq., Charged with

Aiding and Abetting in the Escape of a Fugitive Slave Called Shadrach" contains Dana's eloquent defense in 1851 of the fugitive slave Shadrach's elderly counsel, who was offered up in Boston as a scapegoat on the grounds that he must have conspired in Shadrach's rescue. Dana begins by praising his client and then inveighs irrelevantly against the disgusting Fugitive Slave Law, which he says is fortunately not part of American organic law but is repealable. He then blasts the servility of Bostonians who silently accepted the terms of the law, and protests against the subtle pressures brought upon anyone in Boston who defends a Negro accused of being a runaway slave. He lauds the bravery of Davis, and by implication his own generosity and courage.

In his sketch of the aftermath of the rescue, Dana ridicules President Millard Fillmore himself: "A standing army is to be ordered to Boston. . . . The chief magistrate of fifteen millions of people must launch against us the thunders from his mighty hand" (184). He fires away at his courtroom opponent, United States District Attorney George Lunt, accusing him of laughing at Shadrach's other counsel, Robert Morris, who was the first Negro lawyer admitted to the Suffolk bar.[7] When Lunt denied the charge, Dana shot back, "Do you deny you did so? It was seen and noticed by us all. I spoke to you at the time." Lunt lamely said that he only smiled, that he could not always control his muscles, at which Dana replied, "I am sorry you could not control them on this occasion. It led off and encouraged others, who take their cue from persons in high stations" (208). Best of all, Dana discredits Lunt's two leading witnesses, Prescott and Byrnes.

The whole superb speech, which lasted five hours, has the excitement of a Perry Mason diatribe and in addition a basis in reality. Dana deserves great praise for tackling the power of the reactionary federal government, and his then uncomfortable position has been fully vindicated by history.

"Against the Rendition of Anthony Burns to Slavery: May 31, 1854" was Dana's four-hour closing argument in the Burns case. Accepting the hideous Fugitive Slave Law as constitutional for the time being, Dana vigorously presses for the narrowest possible interpretation of it: "I pray your Honor, earnestly, to confine this record—the venomous beast that carries the poison to life

and liberty and hope in its fang—to confine it in the straitest
limits. It deserves a blow at the hand of every man who meets
it" (225).

Dana restricts his argument to five main points. First, Burns's
supposed owner, Colonel Suttle, inaccurately deposed that his
slave had a scar on one cheek and a cut on his right hand.
Second, Dana capitalizes on the gratuitous and erroneous testimony of Suttle's friend William Brent that he saw Burns in
Richmond on March 20; nine witnesses proved this statement
to be untrue, since Burns was in Boston at the time. Third, Dana
beats down Suttle's "property" right in Burns on the grounds
that, according to Brent, Suttle leased his slave to another person, one Mr. Millspaugh. Fourth, Dana denies the truth of
Suttle's statement that Burns said he was willing to go back:
"If all that we see about us is necessary to keep a man who is
willing to go back, pray, Sir, what shall we see when they shall
get hold of a man who is not willing to go back?" (232). And
fifth, Dana contends that no escape has been proved: "No matter
how the slave got here, if he did not voluntarily escape against
his master's will, unless both these elements concur, he cannot
be taken back" (230).

Having confined himself to the evidence, while at the same
time including effective implicit criticism of the unsavory law
and of the Southerners who are rubbing Massachusetts noses in
it, Dana closes with a plea to Judge Ellis Gray Loring to free
Burns:

> You recognized, sir, in the beginning, the presumption of free-
> dom. Hold to it now, sir, as to the sheet-anchor of your
> peace of mind as well as of his safety. If you commit a mis-
> take in favor of the man, a pecuniary value, not great, is put
> at hazard. If against him, a free man is made a slave forever.
> . . . The eyes of many millions are upon you, sir. You are
> to do an act which will hold its place in the history of Amer-
> ica, in the history of the progress of the human race. May
> your judgment be for liberty and not for slavery, for happi-
> ness and not for wretchedness; for hope and not for despair
> . . . (232-33)

But Dana's fine legal mind and rhythmic rhetoric did not save
Burns.

Other Works

"The 'Grasp of War' Speech: June 21, 1865 [Faneuil Hall, Boston]" is a logical, impassioned, but not ornate speech, delivered only two months after Appomattox. In it, Dana gives cogent suggestions for handling the Negro problem in the defeated South, suggestions which, if followed, would have obviated half of the social and political difficulties which have challenged and distressed Southerners, good and bad, for more than a century since the speech.

Dana begins by stating that the United States was in stupendous armed conflict, that the South was militarily beaten, and that she now lies in the Northern "grasp of war." The North, as military conqueror, has the power and the right to do at once what the public duty and the public faith require. The North should grant all freedmen arms-bearing, land-holding, and voting rights. The right to bear arms is a matter depending upon the Constitution; but, since owning property and voting are rights which in their details depend upon state constitutions, the North should exercise its war power and coerce the Southern states into amending their constitutions. He boldly urges granting the franchise to certain Negroes at once. These words of 1865 are prophetic:

> To introduce the free negroes to the voting franchise is a revolution. *If we do not secure that now, in a time of revolution, it can never be secured, except by a new revolution.* Do you want, some years hence, to see a new revolution?— the poor, oppressed, degraded black man, bearing patiently his oppression, until he can endure it no longer, rising with arms for his rights—do you want to see that? Do you want to see them submit forever, and *not* rise for their rights? No, neither, you say. Well, my friends, who cry "no," if either of those things happens, it is our fault. If they never get their rights, or get them by a new revolution, it will be, in either event, our fault. (251-52)

Dana then explains why President Andrew Johnson, experimentally returning the franchise to certain white men in North Carolina and Mississippi upon their taking loyalty oaths, did not grant it to freedmen as well. It was because, under slavery, Negroes had never been properly educated. Dana elaborates as follows:

Slavery has degraded the negroes. It has kept them ignorant and debased. It has not, thank God, destroyed them. The germ of moral and intellectual life has survived; and we mean to see to it that they are built up into a self-governing, voting, intelligent population. They are not that to-day. They will become so quicker than you think. They do not need half the care nor half the patronage we used to think they did. And the ballot is a part of our educating and elevating process. (256)

These words of a century ago are worth pondering now. Dana saw more clearly into the heart of the Negro problem than most of his contemporaries—and many of ours.

"The Faneuil Hall Address" was read immediately after his "Grasp of War" speech and was enthusiastically received by the audience and later by readers in many parts of the country. It calmly points out that only war forced the Southerners to abandon their policies toward states' sovereignty and toward Negroes. The North must now so act as both to guarantee the eternal supremacy of the federal government and also to assure freedmen that slavery has been forever abolished in America. Before rebel states are readmitted into the republic, their constitutions must extend suffrage to their citizens "in such manner as to be impartial and not based in principle upon color" (269), though not necessarily, of course, universally. Dana astutely sees that already, only two months after surrender, the South is beginning to plan a new and more subtle campaign: "The more recent signs are that the spirit which caused the war is preparing to fight over politically the ground it has lost in battle" (271).

Dana next makes clear, in a passage which should command respectful attention today, that he is concerned not with social but only with constitutional and juridical problems:

Appeals may be made to taste or pride, on the subject of the social equality of the people of color. We must not permit our opinions to be warped by such considerations. The present question is strictly one of political justice and safety, and not of social equality. When the free man of color, educated in the common schools, deposits a vote which he can write himself, gives a deposition which he can read and sign, and pays a tax on the homestead he has bought, the law forces no comparisons between his intellectual, moral, physical, or social condition, and that of the white citizen, of whatever race or nation, who lives, votes, or testifies by his side. (270-71)

Dana plainly saw a couple of generations beyond the Reconstruction miseries which he and many others tried to prevent.

"Enemy's Territory and Alien Enemies: What the Supreme Court Decided in the Prize Cases" is not a speech at all but a pamphlet which Dana published in Boston in 1864, to explain the consequences of the Supreme Court decision concerning the *Amy Warwick* and related prize cases. The heart of Dana's dry brief is the distinction between a *de facto* nation and a *de jure* nation: the factual existence of the Confederacy did not create a legal nation. Dana spells out what the Supreme Court did not decide: mere secession ordinances did not make Southern territory enemy land or its people alien enemies, nor did those ordinances end Southern responsibilities to the federal government. Next Dana summarizes what the Court did decide: in a time of domestic war, the federal government has the right to blockade enemy ports and seize enemy property at sea, under international laws of war. Enemy property is property owned by a person, regardless of his politics, whose residence is in territory held by an organized, hostile, and belligerent power. If all of this commentary seems like legal hair-splitting, it may be comforting to remember that Lincoln's might made it right.

Just before leaving for his trip around the world, Dana attended a meeting to eulogize Rufus Choate, brilliant Boston senator, lawyer, and orator, who once had attacked Dana's stand on the Fugitive Slave Law. In his speech, "Rufus Choate: Remarks at the Meeting of the Suffolk Bar [July 19, 1859] in His Honor," Dana extravagantly lauds the departed genius: he was even-tempered, witty, philosophically potent, masterfully logical, possessed of an acute esthetic nature, and adept in literature and psychology and technical theology. Dana's highly formal remarks are graced by one splendid nautical simile harking back to his seafaring days of a quarter of a century earlier:

... in his [Choate's] presence I felt like the master of a small coasting vessel, that hugs the shore, that has run up under the lee to speak a great homeward-bound Indiaman, freighted with silks and precious stones, spices and costly fabrics, with sky-sails and studding-sails spread to the breeze, with the nation's flag at her mast-head, navigated by the mysterious science of the fixed stars, and not unprepared with weapons of defence, her decks peopled with men in strange customs, speaking of strange climes and distant lands. (289)

"The Monroe Doctrine" is not a speech but a long, two-part essay-note reprinted from Dana's edition of Wheaton's *Elements of International Law*. The first part concerns attempts at colonization of portions of the American continent by European powers; the second discusses European intervention in American affairs. The well-informed, comprehensive note ends with a summary and a bibliography. It is perhaps the best and most influential of the many expansive notes in Dana's Wheaton.

"Argument Before the Halifax Fishery Commission" is the last important speech which the aging, frustrated Dana was obliged to give. As printed by his son in *Speeches in Stirring Times*, the two-part argument comes to almost twenty thousand words and includes testimony from expert witnesses. Dana must have worn out the Commission with his parade of political, commercial, and fishing facts—we have more than four thousand words simply on cod, on mackerel, and on Gloucester markets—but these are brilliantly assembled to show that Canadians should be permitted to sell duty-free their catch of fish in the United States and that in return Americans should be allowed to fish in Canadian waters within the arbitrary three-mile limit.

To vivify his contention that free fishing and free trade would help both countries, Dana effectively uses homely analogies and imaginary dialogue to reduce the complex issues to simpler terms. In short, he once again concentrates all his powers upon a tangled issue, for the betterment of his country. He is tactful, courteous, learned, aptly analogical, remorselessly logical, and—we ought to add—genuinely persuasive. But the Commission was evidently not impartial, and again Dana's efforts went for nought.

Letters to a Son

The letters from Dana to his son Richard Henry Dana, III, printed after *Speeches in Stirring Times*, comprise, as we have noted, the most sizable collection of letters by Dana in print.[8] It is somewhat disappointing, for two reasons: Dana always treated his son as a pupil to be lectured and almost never as a friend with whom to share problems. In addition, the collection is incomplete. However, these letters and most of the extant unpublished ones from Dana to his son are necessarily barren of biographical material for the same reason that letters from other great men to members of their families usually are—the really vital topics are intimately talked over, not written about.

Dana never neglected an opportunity to convert a letter into a preceptive essay. For a dozen years he listed spelling errors in the letters and even the journals of his son.[9] When the lad was nineteen and about to enter Harvard, he was treated to the following from his father, then vacationing on the Isle of Skye off western Scotland:

> Do not get drawn into girls' society. It is possible that you may become, or may think you are, interested in some one. Think what you are to do on earth. Man is meant *to be* and *to do*, and not to be tied down. You have four years of college, and then of a profession,—through all which you must be *free*, to do whatever will be best for your future. . . . If you get into any trouble, by your own fault or by accident, come to me at once. I know and can allow for the temptations of youth; and, surely you need not fear that I shall be hard or unsympathetic. Remember this, and treat me as your *friend* as well as father. (472)

Dana candidly reveals his dominant motive a few times: "I have only a natural desire to see you *perfect*" (488). And again, "You must do all you can to *fit yourself* for the career of a jurist and statesman, so that it shall not be your fault if you are unemployed" (488). Other letters stress the importance of Latin study, good health, promptness in answering mail, the extreme usefulness of the French language (best studied with the help of a tutor), and the like. When young Dana seemed to be spending a disproportionate amount of time rowing stroke on the Harvard crew, the father cautioned him not to neglect his reading or his devotions. And, when the crew lost on one occasion, the boy had this sententiousness for solace: ". . . it may be better for you in the end, not to have been victorious. It is a discipline to your moral character" (474).

Surely Dana should have unbent with the boy and youth,

romped in the grass with him a little, and sent him a humorous letter once in a while. But how did Richard Henry Dana, III, respond? According to his biographer, he "worshipped" his father;[10] and his introduction to the letters praises his father to the skies, as a man ever idealistic, solicitous, kind, and sweet tempered.

IV Journal

Dana's *Journal* has entries of three main sorts: his daily, or nearly daily, running comments on professional and social activities in and not far from Boston; his extensive descriptions of persons, places, and doings while he was on brief pleasure trips in the eastern part of the United States; and finally his often charming accounts of his extensive vacations in England and France in 1856 and then around the world in 1859-60.

As we have seen, Dana fully describes such dramatic personal experiences as his being slugged after the Anthony Burns case and such social institutions as the Saturday Club. In addition, he occasionally worries in his *Journal* about a law case; he carefully tells of meeting Charles Dickens among scores of other celebrities, of conferring politically in smoke-filled rooms in Boston and Buffalo and elsewhere, and of traveling along the Hudson River and in the Adirondacks, to name but two vacation areas he frequented.

It seems logical to conclude that Dana intended to write a book or two (like *To Cuba and Back*) based upon the careful notes he kept during his longer trips. Many of the more exciting, picturesque, and informative events and scenes depicted in the *Journal* make splendid reading just as they are; and readers can only regret that Dana did not continue the record longer and that he did not see fit to record his inner feelings on more subjects. It is unfortunate too that his *Journal* abruptly ends late in 1860, with his return from his trip around the world. If he had gone on with his diary, he could have told us about his personal responses to the coming of the Civil War, to the ascendancy of President Lincoln, and to his work in Washington and his visits to the battlefields just to the south of that city. And, if he had kept his journal for four full decades instead of two, he could have recorded for us his feelings upon being sued for plagiarism, his disappointment at having his appointment as ambassador to England blocked, and his last happy years abroad.

But what we do have is superb. His *Journal* shows Dana to be a man keenly alive to his times, particularly to political currents; a person of relentless, high Christian honor and of keen intelligence, well-trained powers of observation and expression, and great physical stamina; and, finally, a man ever anxious to regard his experiences as a challenge to moral greatness and furthermore as innumerable lessons which he might explain to his family. Unfortunately, he chose to make of his *Journal* only a repository for private comments and notes; he did not intend it for publication as we have it. Therefore it is frequently haphazard and often shapeless. Dana's *Journal* is a kind of fragmentary draft of notes toward an Education of Richard Henry Dana, Jr., but with this difference from *The Education of Henry Adams*: Dana regarded life as a divinely watched struggle from which the morally upright not only should but actually do emerge victorious.

CHAPTER 9

Brief Summary

RICHARD HENRY DANA, JR., was both a better writer than he realized and a less significant lawyer-politician than he aspired to be. From the point of view of most twentieth-century readers, it seems sad that he did not devote more of his titanic energy to literary work and less to his profession. Temperamentally, he was unsuited for the rough-and-ready politics for which America was noted in the period from 1850 to 1880. Ironically, he is known today not because he was an active lawyer and politician but because of one book, which he wrote in large part to bring business to his law office.

Dana's *Two Years Before the Mast* is universally popular. It is an authentic narrative, based upon real-life experiences, realistically told, and hence entirely credible. Circumstances in his two-year "magical chance" were such that his literary account of it has the natural shape of a tree springing from real soil and waving real branches against the sky. Such a book touches romantic springs in all of us. It may be marred by occasional stylistic infelicities, but all the same it will live serenely on. It has many of the archetypal contours of literary masterworks. It is no exaggeration to say that *Two Years Before the Mast* is likely to live as long as any piece of writing that America has yet produced.

It is therefore regrettable that, even as Dana was writing it, and surely when he was deprecating its popularity, he was moving in a direction which took him away from the sailor-boy he so captivatingly immortalized. His two-year Odyssey he too quickly chose to regard as a parenthesis in a life destined for more memorable accomplishments.

Dana began life in Boston under the shadow of a morose misfit of a father, whom, however, he always treated with commendable respect. His yearning for spiritual nourishment was not

satisfied among the conservative Congregationalists to whom his
father was loyal, and after his return from the sea Dana joined
the Episcopal Church. His early schooling was not notable, and
only upon entering Harvard College did he begin to obtain something like adequate intellectual stimulation. It was not until his
return from California that he first demonstrated his manifold
abilities and excelled at Harvard and subsequently in law school.

If, instead of determining upon the profession of law, he had
exploited the staggering success of his first book, he might have
gone on to write our earliest local-color fiction cast in California
or to anticipate Melvillean metaphysics cast upon the waters.
But he chose the law, respectable marriage, and Free Soil politics
—choices that do not decry the man's significant professional
achievements. He was an able lawyer, a keen adversary in de-
bate, an effective lecturer, and an acute political theorist. He
defended the rights of sailors and Negroes; he sought to improve
the machinery of the law, both state and national; he loyally
served his country during Lincoln's administration; and he stood
ready to serve later but was never given a chance commensurate
with his abilities. It must be added that Dana was unable to
make the most of what chances he did have professionally. He
was rigidly righteous, uncompromising, and all too deserving of
his fatal sobriquet—"The Duke of Cambridge."

His minor writings are admirable and deserve more attention
than they have received in the twentieth century. *The Seaman's
Friend* is an informative manual. *To Cuba and Back* is spotty
but also canny, penetrating, and challenging; in addition, it indicates the direction Dana might have taken if politics and personal reverses had not intervened. Since he was observant and
had a fine sensory memory, it seems unfortunate that he never
reworked passages from his *Journal* into publishable accounts of
his travels, especially in England, France, the Orient, and the
Mediterranean area. After the Civil War he published a solid
edition of Henry Wheaton's *Elements of International Law,*
magnificently annotated; but unfortunately this work made a
foe out of its previous editor, who combined forces with Dana's
major political foe, and together they blocked his appointment
as ambassador to England and thus ended his public career.

Time and again Dana took to the lecture platform to urge his
countrymen to protect the laissez-faire system, to befriend the

sailor, to accord the fugitive slave his constitutional rights, to extend freedom across a united America, and to keep religion in the classroom and indeed in American life. We may differ with Dana on many points, but we should all agree that he was honorable, sincere, selfless, and formidable.

Death ruined Dana's private plans to write an autobiography, a history of his family, and a book on international law. Later his son's edition of Dana's major speeches gathered into one impressive volume evidence of his political and oratorical wizardry. His *Journal* furnishes a hundred additional proofs of his skill, devotion to duty, probity, and literary competence.

It is to his one major literary effort, however, which one should most wish to return at last. A boy's work, *Two Years Before the Mast* is also a man's enduring work. Its appeal is varied and undying, since it is a graphic account of the adventuresome, boring, and oppressed lives of real sailors. Confronting new seas and new lands, and mastering arduous tasks, its hero is as ageless as Ulysses and Kilroy. When he stood on the *Alert* deck in Boston Harbor at sunset, his long voyage done and his future uncertain, Richard Henry Dana, Jr., could not know that the ingredients of his fame were all close at hand, in his teeming memory. Decades later, as he lay dying in Rome, let us hope that he willingly let slip all thoughts of his courtroom and lecture-hall triumphs and concentrated instead on the image of a brave lad leaping past his timid mates out onto the bouncing bowsprit with John the Swede.

Selected Bibliography

PRIMARY SOURCES

A. *Bibliographies*

DANA, RICHARD HENRY, III, ed. *Speeches in Stirring Times and Letters to a Son.* Boston: Houghton Mifflin, 1910. Dana's son includes a bibliography of his father's writings, pp. 503-12.

HART, JAMES DAVID. "Richard Henry Dana, Jr." Unpublished doctoral dissertation, Harvard University, 1936. Includes a bibliography of Dana's writings, pp. 473-91.

———. "The Other Writings of Richard Henry Dana, Jr.," *Colophon*, V (December, 1934), Pt. 19 [12 pp.]. Praises Dana's Free Soil speeches, courtroom speeches, edition of Wheaton's *Elements of International Law,* and *To Cuba and Back,* and briefly but excellently analyzes his *Journal.*

LUCID, ROBERT FRANCIS. "The Composition, Reception, Reputation and Influence of *Two Years Before the Mast.*" Unpublished doctoral dissertation, University of Chicago, 1958. Several appendices list editions of *Two Years Before the Mast* (including translations), indicate numerous voyage accounts written after 1840 which resemble Dana's book, list California histories which have made use of it, and list numerous contemporary reviews of it and related material; pp. 220-43.

METZDORF, ROBERT F. "The Publishing History of Richard Henry Dana's *Two Years Before the Mast,*" *Harvard Library Bulletin,* VII (Autumn, 1953), 312-32. Expertly follows the vicissitudes of Dana's masterpiece.

SHAPIRO, SAMUEL. *Richard Henry Dana, Jr.: 1815-1882.* East Lansing: Michigan State University Press, 1961. Contains a thorough descriptive bibliography of Dana's principal published writings, pp. 242-44.

B. *Texts (selective and in chronological order)*

Two Years Before the Mast: A Personal Narrative of Life at Sea. New York: Harper, 1840. (Dana revised this work when the copyright reverted to him, adding a new preface and replacing his "Concluding Chapter" with "Twenty-Four Years After." The result was the so-called Author's Edition, Boston: Fields,

Osgood, 1869. The next important edition was that of Osgood in Boston, 1871, which was slightly revised in 1872 and again in 1876 (for the final time by Dana). The last authorized edition in Dana's lifetime was that of Houghton, Osgood, in Boston, 1879. In 1895 Houghton Mifflin, of Boston, published the 1876 text together with a biographical sketch of Dana by his son, Richard Henry Dana, III, who issued through the same publisher in 1911 a fine edition graced by a valuable introduction and informative appendices. Many inexpensive reprints have been issued. Occasionally, lavish editions have appeared. Both types vary in textual accuracy. The most recent and indubitably the best is the one edited by John Haskell Kemble from the original manuscript and from the first edition, 2 vols., Los Angeles: Ward Ritchie Press, 1964. It includes journal and letter material of 1834-36 and 1859-60. It is intelligently annotated; includes helpful appendices concerning vessels, persons, and nautical terms; is sumptuously illustrated, in part with skillfully chosen contemporary pictures and charts; and has a thorough index.

The Seaman's Friend . . . Boston: Little, Brown and Loring, 1841.

To Cuba and Back: *A Vacation Voyage.* Boston: Houghton Mifflin, 1859. Reprinted, slightly abridged and with a brief Introduction by C. Harvey Gardiner, Carbondale and Edwardsville: Southern Illinois University Press, 1966.

Henry Wheaton's Elements of International Law. Ed., Richard Henry Dana, Jr. Boston: Little, Brown, 1866. The most accessible edition of Dana's edition of Wheaton is that of George Grafton Wilson, Oxford: Clarendon Press, 1936, No. 19, Publications of the Carnegie Endowment for International Peace, Division of International Law, Washington: *The Classics of International Law*, ed. James Brown Scott. This is a reprint of Dana's brilliantly annotated but carelessly proofread edition of Wheaton's classic; its previous editor, William Beach Lawrence, sued Dana for plagiarism.

Circuit Court of the United States, Massachusetts District. *In Equity: William Beach Lawrence vs. R. H. Dana, Jr., et Als.* Boston: Mudge, 1867. Contains Dana's lengthy direct examination, cross-examination, exhibits, and deposition, in connection with his suit for plagiarism by William Beach Lawrence.

Speeches in Stirring Times and Letters to a Son. Ed., Richard Henry Dana, III. Boston: Houghton Mifflin, 1910.

"Journal of a Voyage from Boston to the Coast of California, by Richard Henry Dana, Jr." Ed., James Allison, *American Neptune*, XII (July, 1952), 177-86. The brief sea journal which

Dana kept and on which he based much of *Two Years Before the Mast;* meticulously annotated by the editor. (Reprinted in John Haskell Kemble, ed., Dana, *Two Years Before the Mast,* pp. 365-75.)

"Five Dana Letters." Ed., James Allison, *American Neptune,* XIII (July, 1953), 162-76. Letters from Dana to his aunt, his sister, his brother, and his father, commenting on life at sea, in California, and on first returning to New England. (All but the last of these letters, one to his brother from Newport dated September 23, 1836, are reprinted in John Haskell Kemble, ed., Dana, *Two Years Before the Mast,* pp. 379-95.)

An Autobiographical Sketch (1815-1842). Ed., Robert F. Metzdorf. Hamden, Connecticut: Shoe String Press, 1953. Dana's brief autobiography, which serves as a preface to his *Journal;* expertly annotated.

The Journal of Richard Henry Dana, Jr. Ed., Robert F. Lucid. 3 vols. Cambridge, Massachusetts: The Belknap Press of Harvard University Press, 1968. Absolutely essential to a complete understanding of Dana; expertly edited and with a penetrating, charming "Introduction."

C. *Manuscripts*

Unpublished material by and concerning Dana is to be found in the Massachusetts Historical Society, Boston, Massachusetts: the Longfellow House, Cambridge, Massachusetts; the Women's Archives, Radcliffe College, Cambridge, Massachusetts; the Library of Congress, Washington, D.C.; the National Archives, Washington, D.C.; and to a much lesser extent elsewhere. (For further details, see Shapiro, "References," in *Dana,* pp. 241-42. Also recommended are Shapiro's "Notes," pp. 199-240; they are usually useful but are occasionally hard to follow and are sometimes erroneous.)

SECONDARY SOURCES

A. *Books*

ADAMS, CHARLES FRANCIS. *Richard Henry Dana; A Biography.* 2 vols., rev. ed. Boston and New York: Houghton Mifflin, 1891. The standard nineteenth-century biography; stresses the cultural qualities of Dana but has been outmoded by recent scholarship.

BROOKS, VAN WYCK. *The Flowering of New England 1815-1865.* New York: Dutton, 1936. Smooth but imperfect evocation of the New England atmosphere in Dana's era.

EMERSON, EDWARD WALDO. *The Early Years of the Saturday Club.* Boston and New York: Houghton Mifflin, 1918. Contains a brief, temperate character sketch of Dana, pp. 39-45.

EXMAN, EUGENE. *The Brothers Harper: A Unique Publishing Partnership and Its Impact on the Cultural Life of America from 1817 to 1853.* New York: Harper & Row, 1965. Discusses the publication history of *Two Years Before the Mast* in a light somewhat more favorable to the Harper brothers.

HIGGINSON, THOMAS WENTWORTH. *Cheerful Yesterdays.* Boston and New York: Houghton Mifflin, 1898. Memoirs of a school friend of Dana's and a fellow Bostonian.

LAWRENCE, D. H. *Studies in Classic American Literature.* New York: Seltzer, 1923. In spite of a predictable quota of mumbo-jumbo, Chapter IX—on Dana's *Two Years Before the Mast*—his provocative insights on flogging and Dana's response to it, Dana's attitude toward Hope the Kanaka boy, Dana's tooth-ache, the potency of the hostile sea and Dana's ability to describe it, and the power of onion and potato juice to counter-act effects of the salty sea.

MORISON, SAMUEL ELIOT. *Three Centuries of Harvard.* Cambridge: Harvard University Press, 1936. Contains background informa-tion essential to an understanding of Dana's college years.

PEARSON, NORMAN HOLMES. "Introduction" to Dana, *Autobio-graphical Sketch.* Ed., Robert F. Metzdorf. Hamden, Con-necticut: Shoe String Press, 1953. Analyzes Dana's purposes in keeping a journal, discusses his aristocratic nature and his moral courage, and relates Dana to Henry Adams.

PERRY, BLISS. "Dana's Magical Chance." *The Praise of Folly and Other Papers.* Boston and New York: Houghton Mifflin, 1923. Informal essay on Dana's luck in escaping Boston convention-ality by going to sea in his youth.

———. *Richard Henry Dana: 1851-1931.* Boston and New York: Houghton Mifflin, 1933. The definitive biography of Dana's son; contains valuable information on Dana, especially his relationship with his family.

PHILBRICK, THOMAS. *James Fenimore Cooper and the Develop-ment of American Sea Fiction.* Cambridge: Harvard University Press, 1961. An excellent study of American sea fiction to about 1850. Valuable for Dana scholars because of its demon-stration of critical discontent with satirical, sentimental, comic, and anti-individualistic sea literature before about 1840; also because of its brief but penetrating discussion of Dana's im-mediate influence upon Realism in sea fiction.

Selected Bibliography

PIERCE, EDWARD L. *Memoir and Letters of Charles Sumner.* 4 vols. Boston: Roberts, 1893. Helpful for throwing light on Sumner's personal and professional relationships with Dana.

SHAPIRO, SAMUEL. *Richard Henry Dana, Jr.: 1815-1882.* East Lansing: Michigan State University Press, 1961. Comprehensive, thorough biography of Dana from a political historian's point of view; perhaps marred by the author's certainty that Dana was a failure and by an anti-conservative and anti-Brahmin bias.

B. *Unpublished Studies*

CEDERSTROM, MOYLE F. "American Factual Voyage Narratives, 1815-1860." Unpublished doctoral dissertation, University of Wisconsin, 1932. Concerns commercial voyages (of whalers, China traders, slavers, and merchant vessels), American naval voyages of note, and disastrous voyages; contains a section on the significance of factual voyage literature as background for other literary work (including fiction); relates Dana and Melville but assumes that the latter's largely fictional works are autobiographical.

HART, JAMES DAVID. "Richard Henry Dana, Jr." Unpublished doctoral dissertation, Harvard University, 1936. The best and most comprehensive biography of Dana; supersedes that of Charles Francis Adams.

LUCID, ROBERT FRANCIS. "The Composition, Reception, Reputation, and Influence of *Two Years Before the Mast.*" Unpublished doctoral dissertation, University of Chicago, 1958. Admirably thorough: excellent in every way.

WEIMAR, GEORGE M. "Richard Henry Dana, the Elder, Critic." Unpublished doctoral dissertation, New York University, 1920. Of interest for revealing the kind of literary mind to which Dana was exposed when he was growing up.

C. *Articles*

CLINE, WALTER. "Dana at the Point, Discrepancies in the Narrative," *Historical Society of South California Quarterly,* XXXII (June, 1950), 127-32. Compares Dana's description of San Juan (in *Two Years Before the Mast,* Chapter XVIII) with reality and points out Dana's discrepancies.

COYLE, WILLIAM. "The Friendship of Anthony Trollope and Richard Henry Dana, Jr.," *New England Quarterly,* XXV (June, 1952), 255-62. Three previously unpublished letters from Trollope to Dana show their warm friendship and the similarity of their temperaments; Coyle suggests that Ezekiel Boncassen in Trollope's novel *The Duke's Children* may have been characterized with Dana partly in mind.

GALLERY, DANIEL V. "Too Far Before the Mast," *Colophon* (New Series), II (Autumn, 1936), 60-64. Points out that the longitude printed in the 1840 edition and also in the 1869 edition as 166°45′ W. for the *Alert* on May 22, 1836 (see *Two Years Before the Mast*, Chapter XXX), must be erroneous and suggests 116°45′ W. (John Haskell Kemble, ed., Dana, *Two Years Before the Mast*, p. 279 n. 50, says that the manuscript clearly reads 106°45′ W.)

HART, JAMES D. "The Education of Richard Henry Dana, Jr.," *New England Quarterly*, IX (March, 1936), 3-25. On Dana's Harvard years and his rustication; analyzes his dualism—sailor and Brahmin—and the educative value of his nautical years; ends by wondering whether Dana's eighteenth-century birthright was worth much.

——. "An Eyewitness of Eight Years Before the Mast," *New Colophon*, III (1950), 128-31. Analyzes the rancorous marginal comments on a copy of *Two Years Before the Mast* annotated by former *Pilgrim* clerk John H. Everett, and discusses Everett's prejudiced motives therefor.

——. "Melville and Dana," *American Literature*, IX (March, 1937), 49-55. An early essay showing that any close friendship between Dana and Melville was necessarily precluded by differences in temperament in spite of their mutual love of the sea.

——. "A Note on Sherman Kent's 'Russian Christmas Before the Mast,'" *American Literature*, XIV (November, 1942), 294-98. Deplores the conclusion of Sherman Kent (see below) as radical and suggests that perhaps Dana confused the Russian feast of St. Nicholas, celebrated shortly before Christmas, with the Greek Orthodox Christmas.

KENT, SHERMAN. "Russian Christmas Before the Mast," *American Literature*, XIII (January, 1942), 395-98. Unreliably questions Dana's accuracy in general because of his specific erroneous placing of the date of the Russian Old-Style Christmas eleven days before Christmas (see *Two Years Before the Mast*, Chapter XXVI).

LUCID, ROBERT F. "The Influence of *Two Years Before the Mast* on Herman Melville," *American Literature*, XXXI (November, 1959), 243-56. A cautious examination of the degree to which

Selected Bibliography

    Melville may have used *Two Years Before the Mast* in writing *Redburn* and *White-Jacket*.

————. "*Two Years Before the Mast* as Propaganda," *American Quarterly*, XII (Fall, 1960), 392-403. A substantial essay which aims to show that *Two Years Before the Mast* had no discernible influence on Congressional legislation abolishing flogging on United States naval and merchant vessels.

WINTERICH, JOHN T. "Two Years Before the Mast by Richard Henry Dana, Jr.," *Georgia Review*, IX (Winter, 1955), 459-61. Briefly comments on Dana's straightforward style and on the inaccuracy of the title of his masterpiece.

Notes and References

Chapter One

1. Richard Henry Dana, Jr., *Two Years Before the Mast: A Personal Narrative of Life at Sea*, ed. John Haskell Kemble (Los Angeles, 1964), p. 343. This recent edition of Dana's masterpiece is by far the best and most attractive ever printed. I quote only from it, except when I quote from "Twenty-Four Years After," which Kemble does not reprint.

2. James David Hart, "Richard Henry Dana, Jr.," unpublished doctoral dissertation, Harvard University, 1936, p. iv; Samuel Shapiro, *Richard Henry Dana, Jr.: 1815-1882* (East Lansing, Michigan, 1961), pp. 2-4.

3. John Bigelow, *William Cullen Bryant* (Boston and New York, 1890), pp. 1-2.

4. "A Fable for Critics," in *The Writings of James Russell Lowell* (10 vols., Boston and New York, 1896), IX, 57.

5. April 25, 1860.

6. Quoted by Charles Francis Adams, *Richard Henry Dana: A Biography* (2 vols., rev. ed., Boston and New York, 1895), I, 4.

7. Robert F. Metzdorf, ed., Richard Henry Dana, Jr., *An Autobiographical Sketch (1815-1842)* (Hamden, Connecticut, 1953), pp. 102-03.

8. Thomas Wentworth Higginson, *Cheerful Yesterdays* (Boston and New York, 1898), pp. 20, 22, 23.

9. Hart, "Dana," pp. 54-55.

10. Samuel Eliot Morison, *Three Centuries of Harvard: 1636-1936* (Cambridge, Massachusetts, 1936), pp. 256-57.

11. Quoted from Josiah Quincy, "History of Harvard College," 1840, by Morison, *Three Centuries of Harvard*, p. 256.

12. *Ibid.*, pp. 251-53, 260.

13. Richard Henry Dana, Jr., to Richard Henry Dana, Sr., August 19, 1832; quoted by Hart, "Dana," p. 84.

14. *Ibid.*, p. 86, note 1.

15. "Education," in *The Complete Works of Ralph Waldo Emerson* (12 vols., Boston and New York, 1911), X, 153.

16. Bliss Perry, "Dana's Magical Chance," in *The Praise of Folly and Other Papers* (Boston and New York, 1923), pp. 53-62.

Chapter Two

1. The *Pilgrim* had three officers, three idle hands, four seamen, and five light hands. Built in 1825 at Medford, Massachusetts, she had two decks and two masts, was 87 feet long, 22 feet broad, 11 feet deep, and weighed 181 tons. The firm sailing her was Bryant, Sturgis, and Company, of Boston. See "Appendix," in Richard Henry Dana, Jr., *Two Years Before*

the Mast: A Personal Narrative (Boston and New York, 1911), p. [531].

2. Herman Melville, *Moby Dick or the White Whale* (Boston, 1892), p. 40 (Chapter VII).

3. Melville may have had Sam Sparks in mind when he characterized Billy Budd, also afflicted with a stammer. Note in addition the alliterative similarity of the two names. Melville, however, may not have known Sam's last name.

4. Herman Melville, *White-Jacket or the World in a Man-of-War* (Boston, 1892), p. 131 (Chapter XXXIII).

5. D. H. Lawrence, *Studies in Classic American Literature* (New York, 1923), p. 174. Note the mistakes Lawrence makes. Sam was not toned up by the flogging but became more sluggish. The captain did not display either a new ease in his authority or a sore conscience. No equilibrium was established between captain and crew. And the captain himself flogged Sam; he did not "have Sam flogged."

6. For an indication of discrepancies in Dana's description of San Juan, see Walter Cline, "Dana at the Point, Discrepancies in the Narrative," *Historical Society of Southern California Quarterly*, XXXIII (June, 1950), 127-32.

7. Richard Henry Dana, Jr., to Richard Henry Dana, Sr., December 31, 1835; quoted in James Allison, ed., "Five Dana Letters," *American Neptune*, XIII (July, 1953), 172-73.

8. When she left Boston bound for California in 1834, the *Alert* had four officers, four idle hands, six seamen, and seven or eight light hands. Built in 1828 at Boston, she had two decks and three masts, was 113 feet long, 28 feet broad, 14 feet deep, and weighed 398 tons. See "Appendix," in Dana, *Two Years Before the Mast* (Boston and New York, 1911), pp. [532-33].

Chapter Three

1. Adams, *Dana*, I, 19-20.

2. Richard Henry Dana, Jr., to Richard Henry Dana, III, March 25, 1866, in Richard Henry Dana, *Speeches in Stirring Times and Letters to a Son*, ed. Richard Henry Dana, III (Boston, 1910), p. 547.

3. Dana, *Autobiographical Sketch*, p. 75.

4. Metzdorf, ed., Dana, *Autobiographical Sketch*, p. 107.

5. Richard Henry Dana, Jr., unpublished baccalaureate dissertation, Harvard College, Dana Papers, Longfellow House, Cambridge, Massachusetts.

6. Dana, *Autobiographical Sketch*, p. 78.

7. Hart, "Dana," p. 140.

8. Robert Francis Lucid, "The Composition, Reception, Reputation and Influence of *Two Years Before the Mast*," unpublished doctoral dissertation, University of Chicago, 1958, pp. 15-16.

9. Dana, *Autobiographical Sketch*, pp. 87-88.

10. Adams, *Dana*, I, 27-28.

11. Dana, *Autobiographical Sketch*, pp. 85-86.

12. Lucid, "Composition . . . of *Two Years Before the Mast*," pp. 13-20.

13. *Ibid.*, pp. 30-42.

14. Dana, ["Preface"], *Two Years Before the Mast*, p. xxii.

15. Richard Henry Dana, Jr., to Richard Henry Dana, Sr., February 20, 1840; quoted in Hart, "Dana," p. 144.

16. Richard Henry Dana, Sr., to William Cullen Bryant, June 12, 1839, Massachusetts Historical Society; quoted in Robert F. Metzdorf, "The Publishing History of Richard Henry Dana's *Two Years Before the Mast*," *Harvard Library Bulletin*, VII (Autumn, 1953), 316.

17. Dana, *Autobiographical Sketch*, pp. 88-89, 110.

18. Metzdorf, "Publishing History of . . . *Two Years Before the Mast*," p. 321. For a discussion more favorable to the Harper brothers, see Eugene Exman, *The Brothers Harper* . . . (New York, 1965), pp. 124-40 *passim*. In March, 1841, one of the Harper brothers told Dana that they had "not yet cleared a profit of two hundred and fifty dollars out of the sale of the work" (p. 138).

19. Shapiro, *Dana*, pp. 12, 201.

20. Van Wyck Brooks, *The Flowering of New England 1815-1865* (New York, 1936), p. 310.

21. Robert F. Lucid, "*Two Years Before the Mast* as Propaganda," *American Quarterly*, XII (Fall, 1960), 392-403.

22. *Ibid.*, pp. 400, 401.

23. Shapiro, *Dana*, p. 189.

24. Elmo Paul Hohman, *History of American Merchant Seamen* (Hamden, Connecticut, 1956), p. 25. While aboard the slovenly *Early Bird* on his way to Hong Kong, Dana recorded the following in his *Journal* for March 6, 1860: "Now I have seen forecastle life & sailor's life *from the cabin*, I begin to wonder how I endured it."

25. Dana, *Journal*, December 29, 1842 to January 17, 1843 *passim*. Adams, *Dana*, I, 50-63, reprints Dana's *Somers* letter.

26. An expertly compiled "casebook" on the *Somers* affair is the one by Harrison Hayford, *The Somers Mutiny Affair* (Englewood Cliffs, New Jersey, 1959). James Fenimore Cooper was immediately hostile to Mackenzie. Herman Melville, whose older cousin Guert Gansevoort was the executive officer aboard the *Somers* at the time of the "mutiny" and hanging, later used the case when he wrote *Billy Budd*.

27. Dana Papers, Longfellow House, Cambridge, Massachusetts, contain numerous letters from Dana to his wife in which he first airs his grievances and then apologizes for doing so.

28. Shapiro, *Dana*, pp. 29-31.

29. Richard Henry Dana, Jr., to Daniel Lord, January 26, 1854; quoted in Adams, *Dana*, I, 124-26.

30. *Ibid.*, I, 126.

31. Quoted in Adams, *Dana*, I, 182, 183.

32. Richard Henry Dana, Jr., to Edmund T. Dana, March 2, 1851, Massachusetts Historical Society; quoted in Shapiro, *Dana*, pp. 61-62.

Notes and References

33. *Ibid.*, p. 73.
34. Quoted in Adams, *Dana*, I, 237.
35. Quoted in *ibid.*
36. *Ibid.*, I, 250; Shapiro, *Dana*, pp. 82-83.
37. Shapiro, *Dana*, p. 89.
38. Quoted in Adams, *Dana*, I, 282-83.
39. *Ibid.*, I, 325.
40. *Ibid.*, I, 323.
41. *Ibid.*
42. *Ibid.*, I, 322.
43. Adams, *Dana*, I, 328-29, sketches Varell's unsavory career. Shapiro, *Dana*, pp. 84-94, gives the best account of the entire Burns case. Suttle sold Burns to a slave trader, who resold him to friends of Burns for a profit. He made his way to Boston, where Dana was happy to see him again, in March, 1855. Burns studied at Oberlin College, became a minister, preached in Canada, and died there in 1862. See Dana, *Journal*, March 30, 1855; Adams, *Dana*, I, 345-46.

Chapter Four

1. Quoted in Adams, *Dana*, II, 162.
2. Adams, *Dana*, I, 357-59.
3. Quoted in Adams, *Dana*, II, 78.
4. *Ibid.*, II, 122.
5. *Ibid.*, II, 123-24.
6. *Ibid.*, II, 127.
7. Shapiro, *Dana*, p. 108.
8. Adams, *Dana*, II, 134, 135.
9. Hart, "Dana," pp. 321-23; Shapiro, *Dana*, p. 51.
10. Richard Henry Dana, Jr., to Lily Dana, February 23, 1859, Massachusetts Historical Society; quoted in Shapiro, *Dana*, p. 110.
11. Hart, "Dana," p. 334.
12. Quoted in Adams, *Dana*, II, 176.
13. Hart, "Dana," p. 352.
14. Quoted in Adams, *Dana*, I, 332. Dana often echoes this opinion in his *Journal*.
15. Dana, *Two Years Before the Mast* (Boston and New York, 1911), p. 480.
16. *Ibid.*, p. 476.
17. *Ibid.*, p. 482.
18. Quoted in Adams, *Dana*, II, 197.
19. *Ibid.*, II, 227.
20. *Ibid.*, II, 235.
21. *Ibid.*, II, 237.
22. *Ibid.*, II, 238.
23. *Ibid.*, II, 239.
24. *Ibid.*, II, 240.
25. *Ibid.*, II, 241.

26. *Ibid.*, II, 242.
27. *Ibid.*, II, 243-44.
28. *Ibid.*, II, 246.
29. *Ibid.*, II, 247.

Chapter Five

1. Shapiro, *Dana*, p. 118.
2. *Ibid.*
3. *Ibid.*, p. 119.
4. *Ibid.*, pp. 121, 225.
5. David M. Silver, *Lincoln's Supreme Court* (Urbana, Illinois, 1956), p. 109. See also Clinton Rossiter, *The Supreme Court and the Commander in Chief* (Ithaca, New York, 1951), pp. 69-77.
6. Quoted in Adams, *Dana*, II, 269 (witness not identified).
7. Richard Henry Dana, Jr., to Richard Henry Dana, Sr., May 4, 1864, Massachusetts Historical Society.
8. Richard Henry Dana, Jr., to Charles Francis Adams, March 9, 1863, Massachusetts Historical Society; quoted in Adams, *Dana*, II, 264, 265. See also Shapiro, *Dana*, p. 129.
9. Richard Henry Dana, Jr., to Richard Henry Dana, Sr., May 4, 1864, Massachusetts Historical Society.
10. Richard Henry Dana, Jr., to Richard Henry Dana, III, Easter Sunday [April 16], 1865, Massachusetts Historical Society.
11. Richard Henry Dana, Jr., ed., "Editor's Preface," to Henry Wheaton, *Elements of International Law* (Boston, 1866; reprinted Oxford, 1936), p. viii.
12. Circuit Court of the United States, Massachusetts District, *In Equity: William Beach Lawrence* vs. *R. H. Dana, Jr. et Als.* (Boston, 1867), pp. 308-9. The entire case can be followed in this unpleasant but fascinating book.
13. Quoted in Adams, *Dana*, II, 290.
14. George Grafton Wilson, ed., "Sketch of the Life of Richard Henry Dana, Jr.," in Dana, ed., Wheaton, *Elements of International Law* (Oxford, 1936), p. 23a.
15. Lawrence's lawyer wrote a ninety-page deposition in 1867 on possible parallels between his employer's notes and Dana's. Dana's 1868 defense ran to 222 pages, which Lawrence replied to in 244 vicious pages. Dana then answered in ninety-eight more pages in 1869. The judge, deciding against Dana, turned the matter over to Henry W. Paine, master in chancery, whose report, filed in 1880, covered 211 pages. See Adams, *Dana*, II, 305; Wilson, "Sketch of the Life of Dana," pp. 22a-23a.
16. Dana, "Editor's Preface," to Wheaton, *Elements of International Law*, pp. v, viii.
17. Adams, *Dana*, II, 319-21; Shapiro, *Dana*, p. 157.
18. Adams, *Dana*, II, 321.
19. *Ibid.*, II, 324.
20. Dana, *Speeches*, p. 119.

Notes and References

21. Richard Henry Dana, III, "Introductory Sketch," in Dana, *Speeches,* p. 54.

22. Adams, *Dana,* II, 348; Shapiro, *Dana,* p. 231. Even the Democratic candidate polled almost three times as many votes as Dana.

23. Shapiro, *Dana,* p. 154.

24. Letter of March 15, 1873; quoted in Adams, *Dana,* II, 359.

25. For a biased but thrilling narrative of the dispute, see James Truslow Adams, *The Adams Family* (Boston, 1930), pp. 316-20.

26. James Russell Lowell to Richard Henry Dana, Jr., March 8, 1876, Longfellow House, Cambridge, Massachusetts.

27. Shapiro, *Dana,* pp. 162, 166, 167.

28. Telegram from William M. Everts to Richard Henry Dana, Jr., March 15, 1876, Massachusetts Historical Society.

29. Richard Henry Dana, Jr., to George S. Boutwell, March 16, 1876; quoted in Adams, *Dana,* II, 372-73.

30. *Ibid.,* II, 376 and note.

31. Shapiro, *Dana,* p. 182. See also Richard Henry Dana, III, "Introductory Sketch," in Dana, *Speeches,* pp. 345-54.

32. Letter of April 22, 1873; quoted in Adams, *Dana,* II, 380.

33. Hart, "Dana," p. 438.

34. Adams, *Dana,* II, 383.

35. Sarah Watson Dana, "Diary," "Book of Facts," Volume 47, August, 1880, Women's Archives, Radcliffe College.

36. Adams, *Dana,* II, 385.

37. Letter of late May, 1881; quoted in Adams, *Dana,* II, 385.

38. Richard Henry Dana, Jr., to Anthony Mundella, March 20, 1881, University of Sheffield Library, Sheffield, England; Sarah Watson Dana, "Diary," Volume 15, 1882, January 1, 1882.

39. Wilson, "Sketch of the Life of Dana," p. 24a. I emphasize this matter because Shapiro—wrongly, in my opinion—says (*Dana,* pp. 183, 185-86) that Dana did little but dillydally in Europe in the three years before his death.

40. Adams, *Dana,* II, 387-88; Richard Henry Dana, III, "Introductory Sketch," in Dana, *Speeches,* pp. 62-63.

41. Sarah Watson Dana, "Diary," Volume 15, 1882.

42. Henry James, "The After-Season in Rome" (1873), in *Italian Hours* (Boston and New York, 1909), pp. 270-71.

43. Adams, *Dana,* II, 388.

Chapter Six

1. Lucid, "Composition . . . of *Two Years Before the Mast,*" p. 146.

2. See Hart, "Dana," p. 96; James Allison, ed., "Journal of a Voyage from Boston to the Coast of California, by Richard Henry Dana, Jr.," *American Neptune,* XII (July, 1952), 177-86; Metzdorf, "Publishing History of . . . *Two Years Before the Mast,*" p. 315.

3. In his manuscript of *Two Years Before the Mast,* Dana tells of two

RICHARD HENRY DANA, JR.

drunken Mexican customs inspectors; see Lucid, "Composition . . . of *Two Years Before the Mast*," p. 42.

4. Perry notes this fact in "Dana's Magical Chance," p. 56.

5. Thomas Philbrick, *James Fenimore Cooper and the Development of American Sea Fiction* (Cambridge, Massachusetts, 1961), pp. 115-16.

6. Ernest Hemingway, *Death in the Afternoon* (New York, 1932), p. 2.

7. Hart, "Dana," p. 97. It seems to me that Hart's statement is extreme. It is one thing to praise Dana for "distance" but something quite different to be glad that he was denied access to more material than his memory and his meager notes provided. It is likely that he forgot several important unrecorded events and sensations, the use of which might have improved even the marvelous book he did write.

8. Allison, ed., "Journal of a Voyage," p. 181. Dana awkwardly tells us in Chapter XXX on the way home in the *Alert* of the nightmare a shipmate had on the *Pilgrim* outward-bound a year and a half earlier.

9. Lucid, "Composition . . . of *Two Years Before the Mast*," p. 27.

10. See Kemble, ed., Dana, *Two Years Before the Mast*, p. 167 n. 30.

11. "The Poet," in *Complete Works of Emerson*, III, 9-10.

12. John T. Winterich, "Two Years Before the Mast by Richard Henry Dana, Jr.," *Georgia Review*, IX (Winter, 1955), 460-61.

13. Melville is only being modest when in *White-Jacket*, p. 97 (Chapter XXIV), he commends Dana's book as "unmatchable." Melville outdoes even Dana in danglers. In *Omoo* (New York, 1924) alone I have counted sixty-five of them, including what I nominate as the two best dangling participles in serious American fiction: "Waking the men, the corpse was immediately rolled up in the strips of blanketing upon which it lay . . ." (p. 39 [Chapter XII]); and "Continuing to ply his tool, however, quite energetically [Dr. Long Ghost is rowing], I thought he would improve after a while . . ." (p. 149 [Chapter XLI]). I regard Leedice Kissane as ingenious but misguided when she attempts to justify Melville's several dangling constructions in "Bartleby"; see her "Dangling Constructions in Melville's 'Bartleby,'" *American Speech*, XXXVI (October, 1961), 195-200. A dangling modifier is simply illogical, however clear contextually.

14. Dana would have profited from George Orwell's suggestion: "One can cure oneself of the *not un-* formation by memorizing this sentence: *A not unblack dog was chasing a not unsmall rabbit across a not ungreen field*"; "Politics and the English Language," in *Shooting an Elephant and Other Essays* (New York, 1950), p. 90.

15. The form of some of these expressions, and others like them, should have been regularized during proofreading. Sometimes Dana italicizes them, sometimes he puts them within quotation marks, and sometimes he does neither; in addition, he is inconsistent in hyphenating. Note for example his treatment of "anchor watch," "fandango," "gente de razon," "haze," "hove-to," "knock off," "thick," and "turn-in." According to the *Oxford English Dictionary*, *Two Years Before the Mast* contains the first or second recorded usage of some of these words and phrases.

16. Every careful reader of *Two Years Before the Mast* is confused as to

ships' personnel because of Dana's careless way of introducing his personae. He brings in George Ballmer thus: "I remember an English lad who was always the life of the crew, but whom we afterwards lost overboard . . ." (33). The incident "afterwards" begins three pages later. Other examples are rather numerous.

Chapter Seven

1. Shapiro, *Dana,* p. 9, quotes a letter from B. G. Stimson to Richard Henry Dana, Jr., March 16, 1841, Massachusetts Historical Society, "twitting Dana for saying nothing about 'the beautiful *Indian Lasses,* who so often frequented your humble abode in the *hide house* [pun?], and rambled through those *splendid groves* attached thereto [or] the happy hours experienced rambling over those romantic hills, or sitting at twilight on those majestic rocks, with a lovely Indian Girl resting on your knee.' " On his way to Frémont's Mills, during his second trip to California, in 1859-60, Dana encountered a friend, of whom he wrote in his *Journal,* September 4, 1859: "(A woman here is cook who lived with me sev. months, named Mary Collins (?).)"

2. Quoted in Lucid, "Composition . . . of *Two Years Before the Mast,*" p. 38.

3. This is Melville's term for Redburn's friend Harry Bolton (*Redburn: His First Voyage* . . . [Boston, 1924], p. 225 [Chapter XLIV]). Tom Harris is obviously Dana's immaculate friend, of whom he writes the following: "I would not part with the hours I spent in the watch with that man for any given hours of my life spent in study and social intercourse" (196). But Dana's male ideal was the British sailor Bill Jackson of the *Loriotte* (see 90-91). He is the type-image of which Melville's Jack Chase is another example. Curiously, Virginia Woolf's ideal of a vigorous male, at least as a lover for Victorian-age Orlando, is a kind of Bill Jackson, Jack Chase, or Dana, whose "life was spent in the most desperate and splendid of adventures—which is to voyage round Cape Horn in the teeth of a gale. Masts had been snapped off; sails torn to ribbons . . ."; *Orlando: A Biography* (New York, 1928), p. 252.

4. Lawrence, *Studies in Classic American Literature,* pp. 166-67.

5. Dana's father thought that his son would surely die at sea; see Hart, "Dana," p. 95. It is notable that Dana does not allude to his father specifically in *Two Years Before the Mast* but only generally to letters from home.

6. Joseph Campbell, *The Hero with a Thousand Faces* (New York, 1949), p. 30. Maud Bodkin discusses "The Rime of the Ancient Mariner" as the literary work best illustrating "the Rebirth archetype"; *Archetypal Patterns in Poetry: Psychological Studies in Imagination* (London, 1934), p. 54. Dana avoids mentioning Coleridge's "Ancient Mariner" when he describes a real albatross (see 35). However, a page later George Ballmer falls to a watery death with ropes hanging about his neck like the albatross about the ancient mariner.

7. In answering the call to a temporary life of hardship and danger,

Dana set in motion what Lionel Trilling in another connection calls "the mithridatic function"; "Freud and Literature," in *The Liberal Imagination: Essays on Literature and Society* (New York, 1950), p. 56. By doing what he did, Dana inured himself to greater though different pains later in his life.

8. Much is mythic about the terrible-tempered Frank Thompson, whom Dana never saw sit down while on duty, who was impervious to appeals for sympathy, who was once irrationally mild when he heard whispers about mutiny, and who later was mysteriously destroyed by fever off Sumatra and was buried at sea. For added light on Thompson, see his letters home in Kemble, ed., Dana, *Two Years Before the Mast*, pp. 396-400.

9. The non-intellectual aspects of his stay in California were quietly tempting to Brahmin Dana and thus relate to what Maud Bodkin calls "the Nirvana principle, or death instinct"; *Archetypal Patterns*, p. 71. The Melville behind *Omoo* yielded more happily to this tug.

10. Campbell, *The Hero with a Thousand Faces*, pp. 217, 219.

11. Francis McDermott, ed., Washington Irving, *A Tour on the Prairies* (Norman, Oklahoma, 1956), p. xxxii.

12. Melville, *White-Jacket*, p. 97 (Chapter XXIV).

13. Robert F. Lucid, "The Influence of *Two Years Before the Mast* on Herman Melville," *American Literature*, XXXI (November, 1959), 245-46.

14. *Ibid.*, pp. 246-55.

15. Eleanor M. Metcalf, *Herman Melville: Cycle and Epicycle* (Cambridge, Massachusetts, 1953), p. 68.

16. Lucid, "Influence of *Two Years Before the Mast* on Melville," pp. 246-49.

17. *Ibid.*, p. 249.

18. *Ibid.*, pp. 251-55.

19. *Walden*, in *The Writings of Henry David Thoreau* (20 vols., Boston and New York, 1906), II, 4.

20. For a helpful discussion of form in *Walden*, see Lauriat Lane, Jr., "On the Organic Structure of *Walden*," *College English*, XXI (January, 1960), 195-200. Much of what Lane says concerning *Walden* can be usefully adapted to *Two Years Before the Mast*.

21. A case might be made that Thoreau's *Yankee in Canada* (1866) is closer to *Two Years Before the Mast* than *Walden* is.

22. See Henry Nash Smith, *Virgin Land: The American West as Symbol and Myth* (Cambridge, Massachusetts, 1950); R. W. B. Lewis, *The American Adam: Innocence, Tragedy, and Tradition in the Nineteenth Century* (Chicago, 1955); Kenneth S. Lynn, *The Dream of Success: A Study of the Modern American Imagination* (Boston, 1955); Harry Levin, "Some Meanings of Myth," *Daedalus*, CXXXVIII (Spring, 1959), 228-29.

23. Henry Nash Smith expertly analyzes this change and some of the rhetorical problems attendant upon it, in *Mark Twain: The Development of a Writer* (Cambridge, Massachusetts, 1962), pp. 52-70.

24. "Old Times on the Mississippi" is the 1875 heart—Chapters IV-XVII —of *Life on the Mississippi*, the last half of which Twain completed eight

Notes and References

years later and in a totally different mood. The uneven second part is usually weak, documentary, and factual, even though it is occasionally brightened by reminiscence, anecdote, and satire.

25. Hemingway's Odyssey transpired exactly one century after Dana's began.

26. Ernest Hemingway, "Foreword," *Green Hills of Africa* (New York, 1935).

27. I cannot agree with Carlos Baker when he says that "The relationship with M'Cola produces several . . . degrees of the comic. Often the joke is on Hemingway. From M'Cola's position, bird-shooting, whiskey-drinking, beer-bibbing, and failure to hit a large target through excitement or bullheadedness, were all good jokes"; *Hemingway: The Writer as Artist* (Princeton, 1956), p. 173. I do not think that Hemingway here is such a comic writer as even Dana is; although I regard his anxiety to kill big kudus as ludicrous, Hemingway is not consciously responsible for my laughter.

28. Baker, *Hemingway*, p. 166.

29. My foray into *Green Hills of Africa* bagged no double negatives but did yield three danglers: "Once bled, I started to open him [a reedbuck]"; "Looking up, the mountains looked very fine"; and ". . . being as happy as I could be, it made me feel even better"; *Green Hills of Africa*, pp. 53-54, 160-61, 228.

Chapter Eight

1. Dana's friend William Cullen Bryant witnessed such an execution at Guines, Cuba; see his *Letters of a Traveller; or, Notes of Things Seen in Europe and America* (New York, 1850), pp. 389-93.

2. While in Canton, China, Dana was complimented by a former British consul at Hong Kong for his discussion of the Coolie trade in his *To Cuba and Back;* the man explained that from Dana's book they had taken valuable hints in arranging their regulations in China; *Journal*, March 12, 1860. At Shanghai (April 2, 1860) he was again commended for his book.

3. Richard Henry Dana, III, ed., Dana, *Speeches*, p. 240.

4. Dana recorded in his *Journal* (July 17, 1853) that no less a publicist than Rufus Choate, who attended the Convention, came to him and said, " 'Your speech has been magnificent. It it philosophical, affecting, brilliant, logical, everything'—I stopped him and said, 'Mr. Choate, this is too much. I can't bear it.' 'It is all true. It is such a speech as one hears once in an age' "; quoted in Adams, *Dana*, I, 239.

5. For information to the effect that such unanimity was not really the case, see Shapiro, *Dana*, pp. 36-37. At this point Shapiro finds yet another excuse for waxing critical of Dana, who, "forsaking his clients and pregnant wife, . . . repeated this [Faneuil Hall] speech at Woburn, Chelsea, Lowell, and Lynn" (p. 41). Lowell, the most remote of these four towns from Cambridge, is less than thirty miles away; Lynn, the nearest, is close enough so that Dana would, by speaking there, "forsake" his wife for perhaps

three hours. As for his clients, Dana had a capable associate, Frank Parker, in his office.

6. Richard Henry Dana, III, ed., Dana, *Speeches*, p. 164. Hart ("Dana," p. 207) agrees that gravity here represents the Constitution. I do not.

7. Shapiro, *Dana*, p. 61.

8. Adams, in *Dana*, includes portions of many letters by Dana to various persons but makes no effort to present the letters as such. Bliss Perry, in his *Richard Henry Dana: 1851-1931* (Boston and New York, 1933), quotes a few previously unpublished letters from Dana to his son. Shapiro has carefully gone through masses of unpublished Dana letters and quotes from them extensively, in particular those concerning Dana and politics. Hart and Lucid quote many Dana letters—the latter mainly from those concerning *Two Years Before the Mast*—but unfortunately their fine dissertations are not readily accessible. A large edition of Dana's significant letters is urgently needed.

9. It is amusing that in his *Journal* Dana regularly misspells "medecine," "preceeded," "receeded," "vegitable," and "vegitation."

10. Perry, *Dana*, p. 111.

Index

Index

67, 69; *Cheerful Yesterdays,* 24
Hillard, George S., 67
Hohman, Elmo Paul, 62
Holland, Sir Henry, 75
Holmes, Oliver Wendell, 73, 74
Homer; Achilles (*Iliad*), 133, Calypso (*Odyssey*), 132, Cyclops (*Odyssey*), 132, Nausicaa (*Odyssey*), 133, Ulysses (*Iliad* and *Odyssey*), 132, 166
Hooper, Samuel, Jr., 40
"Hope," 45, 127, 130, 137
Howe, Samuel Gridley, 80
Howells, William Dean, 17, 73, 115
Hugo, Victor, 120
Huxford, Henry, 71-72

Irving, Washington, 17, 20, 75, 108, 134-35, 138, 140; Rip Van Winkle ("Rip Van Winkle"), 133, *A Tour on the Prairies,* 134-35

Jackson, Bill, 134, 136-37, 138, 140
James, Henry, Sr., 73
James, Henry, Jr., 17, 106-07
Jason, 131, 132
John (French sailor), 123
"John the Swede" (*see* Linden, John)
Johnson, Andrew, 97, 157
Johnston, 83-84
Johnston, Mrs., 84
Jonah, 133
Joyce, James; Stephen Dedalus (*Ulysses*), 131

Kalloch, Isaac S., 78
Kamehameha I, King, 126
Keats, John, 28, 107
Kellogg, Ensign H., 103
Kemble, John Haskell, 29
Kilroy, 166

Lagoda (vessel), 39, 40, 49, 126
Lansdowne, Marquis of, 75
Lawrence, D. H., 38-39, 131
Lawrence, William Beach, 94-97, 99,

100, 101, 104
Leech, Samuel, 135; *Thirty Years from Home,* 135
Lesser, S. O., 130
Lincoln, Abraham, 86, 89, 90, 91, 92, 93, 159, 162
Linden, John ("John the Swede"), 33, 38, 137, 166
Little, Brown and Company, 94
Little, C. C., 94
Longfellow, Edith (*see* Dana, Mrs. Richard Henry, III)
Longfellow, Henry Wadsworth, 60, 73, 102; "The Children's Hour," 102
Longfellow, Mrs. Henry Wadsworth (*née* Fanny Appleton), 60
Loring, Ellis G., 156
Loriotte (vessel), 39, 49, 126
Lowell, James Russell, 20, 24, 73, 100, 145, 150; *A Fable for Critics,* 20, *The Biglow Papers,* 145
Lucid, Robert F., 58-59, 61, 108, 118, 135, 136
Lunt, George, 155

Macaulay, Thomas Babington, 75, 88
M'Cola, 141
McKay, Donald, 84
Mackenzie, Alexander Slidell, 63-64
Marsh, George, 45-46, 130, 136
Massachusetts Constitutional Convention, Boston, 1853, 63, 67-68, 89
Massachusetts Historical Society, Boston, 58
Mastiff (vessel), 83-84
May, Harry R. ("Harry Bluff"), 48
Mellus, Henry, 37
Melville, Herman, 17, 30, 38, 84, 108, 109, 123, 125, 127, 135-37, 140, 142, 165; Harry Bolton (*Redburn*), 137, 140, Jack Chase (*White-Jacket*), 136, 137, 140, Captain Claret (*White-Jacket*), 38, 137, Jackson (*Redburn*), 137, Jermin (*Omoo*), 136, Dr. Long

189

Index

73999

818.3
6152